THINK MED|
EGS MEDIA PHIL(

Real Love:
Essays on Psychoanalysis, Religion, Society

Atropos Press
new york • dresden

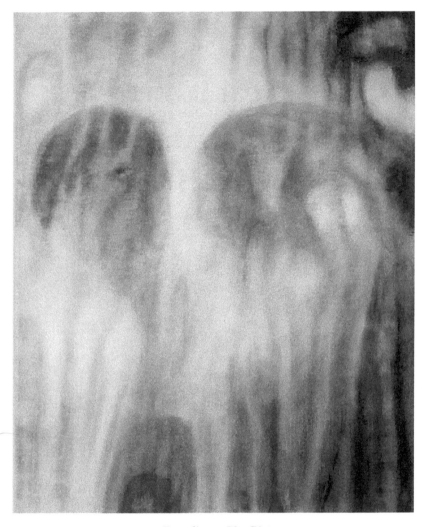

Eurydice n. 53 - Pieta

By Bracha L. Ettinger, 2012-2016, Oil on canvas, 50x41cm. Used by permission.

Duane Rousselle, Ph.D.

Real Love:
Essays on Psychoanalysis,
Religion, Society

ATROPOS PRESS

Copyright © 2021 by Duane Rousselle, Ph.D.
Think Media EGS Series is supported by the European Graduate School

ATROPOS PRESS
New York • Dresden
151 First Avenue # 14, New York, N.Y. 10003
Mockritzer Str. 6, D-01219, Dresden, Germany

Cover/interior design by David/Sunya

Acknowledgements

I would like to thank Bracha L. Ettinger and Ellie Ragland for love and support, Hassan Arif and Alexandre Aubertin for unwavering friendship, Wolfgang Schirmacher, Richard Klein, and Slavoj Zizek for intellectual friendship even when I do not deserve it. I would also like to thank Davide Panagia for continuing to act as an academic mentor for all of these years. This book is also dedicated to JS, JJ, MA, HH, JM, TS, and PP - I hope you find in this an attempt to work my way through the trauma we shared. Thank you to Bracha L. Ettinger for permission to reprint her Eurydice n. 53 - Pieta, 2012-206 - even if we could not place it on the cover. This painting has been very important to the topic. I dedicate this book to Soren Rousselle and Julie Reshe.

TABLE OF CONTENTS

I BELIEF

1. A Love Letter Written to Myself...1
2. What Should We Learn from the Repeated Attacks on Muslims?..............13
3. Love Is Traumatic..22

II CERTAINTY

1. Loving Beyond Possessions...25
2. Sharing Suffering...34
3. Love's Twin Axioms...50
4. Forfeiting Love...58

III COMMUNICATION

1. What Does Sociology Communicate About Love?.......................................63
2. What Is a Code?...69
3. Avoiding the Void...75
4. Talcott Parsons and Pragmatic Sociology..84

IV LOVE LETTERS

1. To Love Is to Be Sick...91
2. Indian Capitalism..106
3. The Saint: A Counterpoint to Mastery...112
4. Love Letters from Sociologists...121

V OVERVIEW OF ARGUMENT..132

BIBLIOGRAPHY..135

INDEX..145

I

Belief

1. A Love Letter Written to Myself

This book contains a love letter written to myself. Alas, it was my fate that in writing to myself I was nonetheless writing it all for you. By feigning to share its contents with you I confess of a belief that one day you might actually read it. This, indeed, is a belief, and it gives rise to a desire to write. I write so that I might finally believe in your existence, and this is not much different from a belief in the existence of God. It is to you and through you that I rediscover God as Other, and, consequently, I construct for myself an enduring social bond. These aforementioned domains (religion, society, and love) are not mutually exclusive. Emile Durkheim, one of the founders of the academic discipline of sociology, already connected God and society when he famously claimed that 'society is God, writ large.' I add to this that love is also constitutive of a social bond and that it partakes in the same object of belief as that of religion. These three categories of human experience relate to an overarching structure of the human experience that orients the subject while initially occluding his or her capacity for reason.

I add the following caveat: if love occludes reason then it is also nonetheless that which provides the enigmatic foundation for an *a posteriori* rationalization. Such is the confusing and paradoxical labyrinth of love. This book does not therefore construct a coherent theory of love since such an effort would serve as a justification of an *a priori* rationalization. Rather, this book explores, in diverse and contradictory ways, some of the various modalities of love today. At its core, a central question is asked: what *is* love? The question should not provoke an epistemological justification or an inquiry into the meaning of love. I am much more interested in the real existence of love. Whereas clinical psychoanalysts often place love in an inverse relation to sex and sexuality (as Jacques Lacan famously put it, 'love is what makes up for the lack of a sexual relationship'), I hope instead to reverse this pessimistic view by locating love at the heart of human existence.

It would seem as though contemporary capitalism has already exchanged the experience of love for that of sex. It is as if the aforementioned Lacanian axiom has become inverted: *sex* is what makes up for the lack of any enduring experience of love. Sex, which was once understood as something 'missing' from a romantic relationship, has now become a compulsory form of enjoyment. It operates within a capitalist discourse by way of substantive, though fleeting, relationships designed in advance to ensure that love can never arise in the first place. Hegel famously wrote that the 'spirit is a bone,' implying that reality is constitutively incomplete and that it is from this primordial incompleteness that the spirit not only emerges but also dwells. Similarly, this incompleteness of reality is that which gives rise to love. It defines the very 'stuff' of an enduring romantic encounter. The name that Lacan gave to this primordial incompleteness is 'sex.' Thus, if sex is that which is incomplete or missing, then today we might claim that 'nothing is missing' in matters of sexuality. Yet, what if love is not only that which arises as a mode of subjective defence against the gaping hole of the missing sexual relationship but also one of the primordial names that we give to the experience of enduring within and beyond that very incompleteness? In other words, what if love is the process of deriving some desire within the incompleteness of existence? In this perspective, then, love is not only the spirit that emerges from the bone — Hegel, in fact, did not claim that spirit *emerges* from the bone — but it is also the fact of something missing of the bone itself.

For further insight into this obscure formulation, we might risk a radical reinterpretation of the Biblical narrative of

Adam and Eve. The English translation of this text could lead one to presume that the first man already had a rib that was subsequently removed and thereafter went missing. It could also lead a reader to presume that Eve was brought into existence from some substantial 'thing.' However, both of these claims have a weak foundation. Adam never had the bone in the first place and Eve was not made out of some pre-existing 'thing.' Rather, what if Eve was created as a symptom to compensate for the rib that Adam was already missing? In other words, what if Eve was quite literally created from a *missing* rib? This would imply that she exists as a phantasmatic compensation for man's primordial solitude. This position is confirmed by Pope John Paul II: "this springs from the depths of his human solitude, which he lives as a person in the presence of all other creatures and all living beings" (1981). It is in this sense that the Biblical narrative can be read according to psychoanalytic theory: from the missing masculine bone the first man installed a desire to fall in love and to therefore partake in the sexual act that gave birth to the social bond: "[i]n this way, the man manifests for the first time joy and even exaltation, for which he had no reason before, owing to the lack of a being like himself" (ibid). The Lacanian claim that 'woman is a symptom of man' therefore aligns well with the Christian narrative since the woman is founded upon man's inability to recognize that he is already lacking from within his very bones. Similarly, the Lacanian claim that 'woman does not exist' aligns with the feminine perspective since it was from something that was already missing within the masculine symbolic universe that initially gave rise to her.

The task of psychoanalysis was once to investigate the unsatisfied or impossible desires of analysands and to assist them in their movement toward some awareness of the structure of their desire and push of their drives. Today things are quite different: the role of psychoanalysis is to install a movement by bringing hitherto lacking desires into play. In other words, the role of psychoanalysis today is often to produce desire itself. If Lacan defined desire always as a 'desire to desire' – which means that it is related to lack – then today, in most cultures around the world,

3

that lack is itself lacking. In other words, desire itself is missing. From the very beginning there no longer seems to be a desire to desire since it has now been replaced with a *need* to desire. This need pushes the subject toward the creation of a lack that has hitherto been missing. Paradoxically, the goal is no longer to make the analysand aware of impossibilities but rather to install and make peace with fundamental impossibilities. At no time has the old French political slogan to 'be realistic, demand the impossible' been more poignant. Take the following example: I have noticed that when I place myself into a quiet room for the purposes of writing or sleeping there will henceforth be no possibility of either writing or sleeping. What is required is the ability to complain: it is only when I am able to complain about distractions or interruptions to my work or sleep that I can install within myself the desire to write or sleep. A television remains on during sleep time, or I work at a noisy café. In both cases I permit myself the possibility of remaining unsatisfied with the noise so that I might simply orient myself with respect to my desire to work or sleep.

These sorts of impossibilities have nothing whatsoever to do with traditional epistemological questions. This was Kant's problem: he sought to define the epistemological scope of an impossibility without recognizing that the impossibility is the mainspring for any epistemological judgment. Thus, the question animating this book was never 'what does it *mean* to fall in love?' since this would imply that love is reducible to its meaningful inscription. Yet, the inscription of love, its writing, is only one moment within an overall process of a love event. Why is it that whenever the question of love arises, we seem to be interested exclusively in its meaning? We ask about the meaning of love with the same intensity and interest that we attempt to hunt down the meaning of life or the meaning of God. At this level, by asking the question in this way, we have only understood too much, and far too soon. I aim to suspend the question of meaning by conducting an investigation into the very 'stuff' of love (which may or may not give rise to meaning). The 'stuff' of love pre-exists its various meaning-laden determinations, it pre-exists as mere potential via rudimentary 'material' capable of installing meaning in the first place. Moreover, it pre-exists precisely in the form of an impossibility at the level of sexual reality. However, in claiming this I do not mean to reduce love to lack and to thereby invert its place within the Lacanian conceptual couple of 'sex' and 'love.' It is more fruitful to claim that love is related to the fundamental lack constitutive of being itself, as lack-of-being or lack-in-being, related, therefore, to an incompleteness within the field of being itself, which installs itself as a solution to that very problem.

I am tempted to discuss the processes of love. Love must be transported in some way from being toward meaning, from navel toward the body which surrounds it. It seems at times that love is located somewhere within the endless disjuncture of meaning and being, of body and navel, even and especially when it seems as though body and navel are one, being and meaning overlap, and so on. The latter pair of 'body' and 'navel' is being used here to facilitate a connection with the Freudian notion of the dream-work, although its conceptual bravado is such that we can derive a lot of mileage: a body is not only this physical body, it is also the knowledge, the codes, the images circulating within a discourse. Thus, we may speak about the 'body of knowledge,' or 'body of communicative codes,' and so on. In any case, Freud claimed that the intelligible components of a dream – its latent symbolic determinations which are to be derived out of the manifest content – run up against a remarkable limit. He named this limit the 'dream's navel' in order to intimate its centrality for the body of dream elements. The navel of the dream is that which resists symbolization, absolutely. I claim that love is there at that zone of unintelligibility marking the navel of all meaning: love occurs where the body loses itself, where the rib was already missing.

Thus, I am really asking how it is that a subject responds to a disorienting trauma surging forth from within his very being. Love is a process of transportation from the solitude of the man (who is one body all alone), toward the construction of another to whom he may dedicate so much of his self-love. Within the navel of his body something pushes outward, puncturing a hole in the consistency of his understanding, something which provides him the possibility of symptomatic responses. And here, within the body of this text, after two years of researching the topic of love, it finally occurred to me that I was endlessly led astray. All of my various theories approached a limit. I was led to conclude that love is multi-dimensional and/or incomprehensible, that it could be anything and yet nothing at all. Indeed, it seemed to me that it was both. Love consists of that movement which tenuously connects reality with knowledge. The following became obvious: being led astray on the path to an answer concerning the question of love was itself the answer I was forced to accept. Love pushes the subject to look astray from the navel toward the consistency of the body.

I am really asking two questions. On the one hand, what is the 'stuff' of love? This requires a complicated response. On the other hand, there is the more particular question: what is a subject's relationship to the question of love today? If the former question causes confusion in some readers then it is most likely because it seems chained to the various possibilities of the latter: a subject may suffer from *certainty* in love though it is also possible that a subject suffers from *doubt* in love. Any general theory of love must take into account the situated experiences of individuals, and, from those cases, and only from those cases, it may find the authority to extrapolate to the wider culture. Whereas we would expect the rise of certainty in love to be related to the rise of cultural psychosis, we would nonetheless expect the prevalence of doubt in love to be related to individual cases of neurosis. It is also possible – and, indeed, there are other possibilities not mentioned – that a particular subject suffers from endless *dissatisfactions* in love. Thus, at the level of the subject we can speak of various structures of love, but at the level of the culture there is nonetheless a structure of love which gives rise to a prevalence of responses within particular subjects. Indeed, it is discourse – another name for the social bond – which gives birth to the cases from which we extrapolate. This is why any general theory of love is doomed to fail, and why, at the same time, we can nonetheless say something general about love. Whereas the love orientation occurs differently according to particular clinical structures, love itself, as a possibility, emerges only as a response to particular traumas at the core of being.

Nowhere has the idea of a miracle and a trauma been so obviously linked than in the world of love today. Love is what simultaneously compels and torments the subject. We run after love just as we run after truth. Although there is a being to love there is also the necessity to respond to this being through the establishment (and sometimes it is the endless tenuous reestablishment) of desire. To illustrate this point, we might turn to the popular narrative of the three wise men within the Christian tradition. Within the darkness of the sky, suddenly, one locates a star. Unlike the other stars, this one moves. The three wise men follow this one star to discover a new body: the king, baby Jesus. The Bible has written, as follows:

> After Jesus was born in Bethlehem in Judea, during the time of King Herod, [wise men] from the east came to Jerusalem and asked, 'where is the one who has been born a king of the Jews? We saw his star when it rose and have come to worship him.' [...] [T]hey went on their way, and the star they had seen when it rose went ahead of them until it stopped over the place where the child was. When they saw the star, they were overjoyed. (Matthew, 2: 1-12)

The purpose of this star was precisely to orient the men toward a common goal, and to, through that goal, construct a shared body of beliefs vis-a-vis the body of the Other in Christ. It is not for nothing that the word star is linked also with the word for desire: *de sidere* means 'from the stars.' What is most real about the stars for people at this time was that they always returned to the same place. Indeed, this point was made by Lacan in his third seminar on psychosis: 'the real is that which always returns to its place.' Within Christianity there is the additional possibility of something that *doesn't always return to its place*. This is the miracle of Christianity: there within the real – as that which always returns to its place – something else goes missing, a star begins to move out of its place. It wasn't until the body of Christ was discovered that the star returned to its place, as if its duty had been completed and it exchanged itself for a body. A body here emerged from within the real itself. It was this certainty, the body of their new desire and common orientation that gave cause and truth to them, and it was explained to them within a dream whose lesson was: do not return to your place, do not return to King Herod. Finally, the cause of the King was exchanged for the cause of their new body, Jesus, to whom they sacrificed their most precious of treasures.

I claim that to love is sometimes also to desire. It is not as Lacan often claimed that love is that which extinguishes desire by prematurely giving it what it seeks. Love is not always the traumatic fulfillment of desire since it can also be the establishment of a zone of non-fulfillment. Love compels the subject toward research: he searches and searches again and again. It is also the zone of invention since, by way of love, the subject invents for himself the miracle of subjectivity, though love also implements a mode of subjective torment: the wise men nonetheless gave up their treasures to the new king. Thus, love is different to different people, and different according to the precise social bonds. Similarly, we would expect it to be different according to religion. Those who seek a comprehensive and cogent theory of love have already fallen too much in love with their own presuppositions on love. I offer the possibility for fresh new confusions. Yet, at the same time, I offer the possibility of profound new certainties and innovative bodies of knowledge. Indeed, today's new torments in love arise from a doubt that is displaced onto the other: for all of our certainty, it is the other who is confused about love, and we are merely engaged in endless attempts to either convince the other of the sincerity of our love or else to give up on love entirely.

Amidst all of these confusions there are some orienting principles. One of my major objectives is to rescue the category of love from a series of ideological distortions. These distortions occur by way of secondary psychoanalytic interpretations, contemporary sociological theories, and naïve religious presuppositions. First, psychoanalytic interpretations often find love to be reducible to matters of transference. In a way, love becomes a clinical roadblock, or the name for a common pathology. We love as a substitution for underlying anxiety, so that the clinical move is to see unconscious motivations that have not yet been properly addressed. Second, contemporary sociological theory derives from the category of love a system of binding individuals together. This was Niklas Luhmann's position in his famous *Love as Passion* wherein he argued that love operates according to a universal semantic logic grounded upon singular communicative codes. Each system has its own binary code distinguishing itself from other self-referential bodies of information. Hence, put simply, the system of love interprets the world according to whether that information is *love* or *not love*. Classical sociological theory had a similar point of view. For the classical sociologists, love was to be understood as a social form or social fact existing independent from subjective life. Georg Simmel even indicated that the overwhelming experience of love requires the development of zones of secrecy; but is it not this domain of secrecy that provides the subject with the breathing room for love to endure? Love as secrecy therefore operates as a solution to the overwhelming proximity of the social bond itself. We fall in love precisely to fall out of the social order. Finally, naïve religious discourses have often celebrated a Christian variant of love, but without realizing it. The discourse of Christian love is so pervasive today that we can see its structure replicated also in popular Jewish, Islamic, Buddhist, and Hindu media representations. When the Christian-secular world represents other discourses it does so only through a sort of dupery: they must love in the same manner as the Christian loves. Christianity has the last word on matters of love today and we are constantly tempted to repeat this pathology. The love of one's neighbour is narcissistic at its core and cannot but arouse deep hatred, since to love the other is always to love him or her 'as thyself.' Agape love – selfless love – remains a fantasy of Christianity except when it reaches its discursive transformation, its conversion, into an altogether different religious discourse.

I see the following temptations, which are to be rectified within this book. First, psychoanalysis often claims that love is an escape from the truth of castration into the imaginary transferences. To love is always to desire to be loved rather than to move through the anxiety of the subject's real truth as symbolic castration. For some psychoanalysts, then, love is what emerges as an imaginary compensation for the fact of a symbolic castration which produces real anxiety. However, it is clear that today our task is not simply to render conscious hitherto submerged symbolic truths, and it is not simply to work our way through and beyond the transferences. Moreover, our task is not simply to interpret the dreams of analysands. The problem is that transferences and dreams rarely exist within today's clinic. We should no longer begin with the assumption that love is a pathology which must be exterminated.

The second temptation is to rush toward the sociological understanding. Yet, the problem is that love is always seen as a favourable social bond. If psychoanalysis tends to place love within a negative register (as an obstacle to a cure) then sociology often places it within a favourable one (as a cure to social obstacles). Lacan claimed that discourse is a social bond, that, in other words, the two are equivalent. The sociological position converges with the psychoanalytic one only when the former is understood not as a system or body of communication grounded upon a central code. We must amend this position by including within it the following psychoanalytic supposition: there is something which interrupts and challenges the phallic code that is at the navel of the body of communication, and this something never stops not being written. One possible name for this something that never stops not being written is love, real love. When I write about real love I mean to align it within the register of the Lacanian category of the 'real,' as that which 'never stops not being written.' What is most real about the Lacanian real is the fact of its love: there is something from within the real miraculously giving rise to subjectivity itself. Love is therefore not only a social bond but it is also that which gives rise to subjectivity as an obstacle to the social bond.

Finally, the most problematic temptation is the third one. The temptation is to give way to the mainstream discourse which invites the subject to flee from the anxiety of love by moving toward the dominant Western ideology on love. This clearly places us in the grips of Christian secularism. I hope that the reader will not be fooled by this name – Christian secularism – since, structurally speaking, there is no other type of secularism. I contend that all attempts to locate an Islamic secularism, Hindu secularism and so on, or to locate secularism before the emergence of Christianity, are ideological traps. Structurally speaking, secularism is Christian, and, moreover, it is the dominant ideology of today's neoliberal capitalism. The perverse belief that love consists of an attitude of tolerance vis-à-vis a neighbour whose differences may be managed, mitigated, or respected by an opposing party is best summarized in the golden rule to 'love thy neighbour as thyself.' It is true that secularism could be located before the introduction of the Christian religion and its textual history, yet was it not because of the secularist attitudes of Christ and his followers that he was capable of emerging as their Lord? Thus, his name, Christ, meaning 'anointed' or 'consecrated' one, similar in effect to the anointing done in Hindu traditions, is itself a mark of his primordial divinity. He was divine before he even had a body. The love of God is the process by which a body is formed from within the real as an inherent potential.

Secularism is what is most Christian about Christianity, and it is through Christianity that any preceding secularist convictions may be properly secured in a body. It is imperative that we conclude that Christianity is only one possible modality of love, one which discretely elevates itself to a culturally dominant attitude: one loves the neighbour *as oneself.* The move is to make use of the *content*, the love of differences, to perpetuate the *form* of a similarity, Christianity. What are we to make of the love of non-Christians, and why is it that we continue to witness Christian principles of love emerge during today's most pressing global/cultural catastrophes? For example, a structuralist reading of the popular image of the woman (without a hijab) hugging a Muslim woman (with a hijab) would be to claim that its text ('this is your home and you should have been safe here') should include the following sub-text ('so long as you respect differences in the same way that we do!'). I merely raise the question: do Muslims fall in love in the same way that Christians fall in love, or is there, finally, a difference in the structure of the Islamic social

11

bond which constitutes love in an altogether different register? Are we to believe that love is a universal category of human experience that functions the same for everybody, irrespective of their demographics or the unique configuration of discourse that marks their social and cultural discourse? Put another way, shall we conclude from this that Muslims, Hindus, Jews, and others are doomed forever to partake only in the ethos of Christian secular love while missing the unique opportunities afforded to them by the structure of their own social bond? How can Christianity get the last word on love when Islam teaches that it alone is the last chapter in the Abrahamic trilogy?

Indeed, Islamic social bonds open up a possibility for an altogether different and perhaps revolutionary perspective which does not perversely disavow love like in Christian secularist versions. Rather, Islamic love seems to project a certainty from which the lover as subject remains in fidelity. This is why Kierkegaard's position on love motions toward the completion of the Christian project of love. For Kierkegaard, mature love always consists of a passage through the intermediary of God: 'God is the middle term [...] only by loving [him] above all else can one love the neighbour' (Kierkegaard, 1847: 57). Kierkegaard recognized that the love of the other is preceded by the love of the universal, such that, perhaps, one should first become honest about the universal before concluding that Christian love is purely relativist and focused on difference as such. This is the starting point for Islamic scripture. How could we not find within the following passage from Kierkegaard the position of a delusional subject in search of universal certainty, whereby differences are not sought but are rather completely eroded?

> Without a 'you' and an 'I' there is no love, and with 'mine' and 'yours' there is no love, but 'mine' and 'yours' (these possessive pronouns) are, of course, formed from a 'you' and an 'I' and as a consequence seem obliged to be present wherever there are a 'you and an 'I.' This is indeed the case everywhere, but not in love, which is a revolution from the ground up. The more profound the revolution, the more

completely the distinction of 'mine' and 'yours' disappears, and the more perfect is the love. (Kierkegaard, 1847: 266)

Kierkegaard retains the singularity of subjectivity by proclaiming a 'you' and an 'I,' but disbands with a notion of ownership by refusing the categories of 'mine' and 'yours.' From this he empties the content of God's creation of bodies and asserts from the hole of 'being' a form of love: it is both singular and universal.

2. What Should We Learn from the Repeated Attacks on Muslims?

We must be critical of the way that Western secular thinking reasserts global dominance through the media, including our participatory social media, in the most cunning of ways. Against the deceptive universality of secular ethics, we should not be afraid to see within Islamic religious discourse the potential for the formation of an honest universality: rather than safeguarding the particularity of a distinctive social group, and rather than elevating itself against that which it pretends to tolerate, Islamic religious ethics seeks a common point of departure among all Abrahamic faiths. The problem is that secularism (e.g., as toleration of Islam) produces an inescapable bifurcation, concealing an unacknowledged intolerance. In this case, the secular frame eclipses possible non-secular Islamic positions. We should be very careful not to fall into the trap of presuming that the incompatibility among the two positions is based simply upon a war between secular relativism and fundamentalist universalism. It is not that secularism is inherently relativist while Islam is inherently fundamentalist. There can be no secular relativist discourse which does not by necessity elevate itself to the universal frame while thereby producing its own phantasmatic point of exception. Within secular discourse, then, it is typically Islam that operates as that point of exception: the latter often becomes codified as fascist, fundamentalist, totalitarian, or hegemonic.

I mean by 'honest universality' that Islamic religious discourse does not pretend that it is concerned primarily with a respect for difference. Any respect for difference is often betrayed by a secret demand that the other also respect difference and this maintains the existing discursive hegemony. The deception is as follows: secular relativism does not at all step outside the problems of hegemonic universality except by way of appearances. Despite its posturing, secularism is not essentially a relativist position. It is perhaps the most ruthless of all of the universalist positions currently in existence. It is precisely by proclaiming tolerance for all that the secular position secures for itself the last word on universality. The initial problem is thereby renewed in a purer form: the accusation against Islam is that it is a problematic universal position, and yet, secularism itself consists of a fundamental problem of universal declarations. If relativism were put to the test by confronting another universal framework then its inadequacies become exposed: the relativist can either quietly elevate his own discourse while simultaneously subsuming the competing discourse, or else the relativist can allow his own discourse to be subsumed beneath the overarching competing discourse. In either case, the final result is a new universality. This is why secularism only appears to have surpassed the problem of fundamentalism even though its underlying fundamentalist universality has only been obscured and its problems exacerbated.

Clinically speaking, there is a name for this discursive logic: 'perverse disavowal.' At its core, so-called Islamic fundamentalism does not function according to the logic of perverse disavowal. Christianity, as one of the world's most popular religious social bonds, is among very few religions to operate according to the perverse logic (see Žižek, 2003). It is the only Abrahamic religion to distance itself from itself in order to achieve universal resurrection. Christians believe that Jesus died for the sins of 'all of humanity,' a death which moves from a particular individual to the renewed universal community of the 'holy spirit.' It is the golden rule from the New Testament and the book of Leviticus that animates Christian ethics. Indeed, to 'love thy neighbour as thyself' bolsters for many Christians an attitude of universal tolerance vis-à-vis difference. Islamic religious discourse moves in an altogether different dimension. It begins with an acceptance of universality via the notion of tawhid (oneness), as exemplified in Surah al-Imran (64): 'Oh, people of the book, come to common terms between us and you!' This is a declaration of the universality of belief itself, and it sustains the proliferation and intensification of sects. Thus, whereas Christianity begins with an admittance of sectarian possibilities and motions toward a renewed universality, Islam begins with the acceptance of oneness, and this gives rise to a proliferation of sects.

This indeed is the only explanation available for the fascinating opposition between Christianity and Islam on the question of sectarianism. A beautiful statement of sectarianism was once offered by T. S. Eliot, a Christian: the only way to keep a religion alive is to perform a sectarian split from its main corpus. Is this not the final lesson of Christianity regarding the question of sectarianism? Yet, conversely, for Islam it functions in precisely the opposite direction: everywhere in the Islamic Middle East there is the charge of sectarianism, and by who other than, precisely, the most radical sects! Thus, we might reverse T. S. Eliot's claim that the only way to keep a religion alive is to perform a sectarian split by claiming that for Islam the way to keep the religion alive is to perform a return to the tradition which united Muslims. Indeed, this accounts for the growth of so-called 'political Islam' as well as the birth of the modern Salifiyah movement: it was a call to return to the tradition of the prophet and his companions. And it is in this way that new sects, whether radical or non-radical, were born in the name of universal Islam. Thus, from a structural perspective, once again, we cannot speak about sectarianism within Islam in the same way that we speak about it in the Christian-secular world. Clearly, a different logic is at play.

If we were to complete our Abrahamic trinity, we would also add that Judaism discovers beneath the apparently tolerant face of the neighbour a monstrous aggression or persecution which necessitates a retreat into the particularity of a social bond. Therefore: the Christian tolerates the neighbour by secretly elevating himself above him, Islam rejects the neighbour by

15

accepting him within the a priori Ummah (the common bond of all believers), and Judaism sees within the neighbour something uncanny and unacceptable within Judaism itself. A simple ideal-type – the methodology of Max Weber, a forefather of German sociology – shall help us navigate this trinitarian labyrinth with *verstehen* (empathetic understanding). Let us take as a preliminary example the case of Abraham. The Jewish faith finds within this prophet the person responsible for rediscovering and making conscious a G-d whose laws were previously repressed and who, like the prophet Moses, received symbolic commandments. Abraham's covenant with G-d was every bit as symbolic as Moses' (who had a more literal tablet). Consequently, there was a rejection of idolatry because any image of G-d obscures the essential symbolic function of the Father's law. No wonder Lacan, in his early 'return to Freud,' outlined, in his 'Schema L,' an imaginary obstacle to the symbolic inscriptions of the unconscious. Lacan was here at his most Jewish, and, indeed, at his most Freudian. He did not yet make a name for himself, since to do that he would be required to experience the loss of his symbolic G-d. In any case, this is the introduction of the symbolic unconscious as that which must be interpreted, deciphered, explored, and revealed by the analyst. And it was Freud's major task to reveal it.

On the other hand, Christians often claim that Abraham is the father of all of those who have faith, irrespective of circumcision. We find this also in the story of Paul, who, by proclaiming the ultimate message of universal tolerance – 'there is neither Jew nor Gentile, neither slave nor free, nor is there male or female, for you are all one in Christ Jesus' – rendered himself an exemplary Christian. Finally, within Islam, Abraham represents only one prophet in a chain of prophets whose existence remains a tribute to the commonality of belief and the various detractors from the straight path. This 'straight path' is itself ingrained in the being who speaks by God, since it is by God that we are born Muslim and due to circumstances – the circumstances of the wider society and social bond into and through which we are born – we are led astray. Hitherto unmentioned here is the case of Hinduism, that fourth great world religion and social bond. It seems to me that

Hinduism and Christianity form a pair, yet moving in opposite directions: in Christianity there is a perverse movement toward that which accepts castration, only to renew disbelief in castration, yet in Hinduism there is a retreat into idolatry in the real.

Between Islam and Christianity, then, Hinduism functions to return the missing symbolic castration within the real. If Christian secularism breeds capitalism (an argument I have made in another book; see Rousselle, 2019) then we see within India not a regress from capitalism but its acceleration. This logic was best expressed to me by a woman from Mumbai who warned me: 'In India, everything is reduced to its packaging, so it doesn't matter what is inside, there is only *outside*.' The problem is not therefore that India is slowly 'developing' and therefore trailing behind 'modern capitalism,' but rather that, due to its ancient traditions and Vedic texts, it has already surpassed modern capitalism. Indeed, Hinduism is inherently both monotheistic as well as polytheistic, even more than Christianity, such that you can choose your God based upon your situatedness within various regional social bonds. In Pune, the social bond celebrates Lord Ganesha, and in another region, there is the celebration of his father Lord Shiva. Lord Ganesha was beheaded by his father, Shiva, and holds within his hand a symbol of his castration: a broken tusk. When the symbolic has not taken hold properly, it returns with force as an image within the real – animals with broken tusks rather than humans with castration anxiety.

The overwhelming intensity of the social bond in India leads one to meditation. No wonder Osho, the celebrated mystical religious leader from Pune, who so often enjoyed festivals and sexuality, was nonetheless forced to introduce meditative practices as the cornerstone of his teaching. The festival culture of India is no different from the capitalist celebrations we see performed on the television screen within the West. Take, for example, Ellen DeGeneres who so often is forced to shelve her sadness and mourning so that she can dance again every day for her audience. Who would want to live in a world where the only rival to the loss of happiness is the possibility that one must be happy and enjoy oneself? A model from India informed me that she never likes to leave her home, especially during the time of religious festivals. The celebrations are overwhelming, and she finds herself suffering from enjoyment. She much prefers to hide away in the quietness of her apartment. Structurally speaking, is this not also a form of meditation? In every case, the meditative practices of India function to construct some distance from the intensity of an over-proximate social bond; some distance, then, from the imperative to enjoyment oneself and to therefore suffer from enjoyment itself. This same distance is produced within Christianity via secular politics: government produces the distance that meditation introduces in India.

In any case, let's return to our Abrahamic trinity: Judaism founds a symbolic Father through his inscription of the law, Christianity founds an imaginary father whose body is sacrificed and then resurrected as universal, and Islam founds a real father who, paradoxically, is not a father at all. Indeed, the vast majority of Muslims refuse to use the word 'father' because this would bring to mind a gendered *this-worldly* body whose biology betrays his transcendental nature. This is why such popular Islamic preachers as Zakir Naik refer to Allah (swt) as 'uncreated.' The real God of Islam is represented also in Surah Qar, aya 16: '[God] is closer to you than your jugular vein.' This is no doubt reminiscent of Jacques Lacan's oft-quoted expression that the unconscious is what is 'in you more than you.' But this time we have an additional twist. We are not dealing with the symbolic unconscious of Judaism nor with the Imaginary unconscious of Christianity. How can we not find in this movement from the Freudian symbolic unconscious, to the imaginary unconscious of Lacan ('be wary of the image!'), a final moment in the real unconscious of Jacques-Alain Miller and the teachings of the 'late' Lacan? The movement is from a Jewish Atheist named Freud, to an Atheist Christian named Lacan, toward, finally, the unspeakable and blasphemous third.

Judaism is perhaps the only religious social bond which has truly accepted the law of the father. As an effort against the jouissance represented by the 'thunderous roar of G-d,' the community remained at a distance from Mount Sinai, circulating around the mountain in fear. There was at least one, Moses, who went to the top of the mountain and delivered the symbolic law to the community. In Judaism, one from the community *ascends* toward the symbolic, demonstrating that the entirety of the religious community requires *at least one* to anchor itself symbolically. It is curious that within Judaism atheism is permitted provided that one is already Jewish. On the other hand, Christianity functions through subjective ambivalence: the community of Christians, gathered together through the 'holy spirit,' exists as a residue of the convergence of the symbolic God with his own image, and this, precisely, is what forms the trinitarian structure. The Christian subject is reducible to this residue, reducible, that is, to what Lacanians refer to as *objet petit a*. The *objet petit a* as object cause of desire functions as agent of Christian religious discourse. Belief is founded upon a prior moment of radical doubt, and this is a theme demonstrated clearly in the narrative of the 'dark night of the soul,' whereby inadequate belief confronts radical doubt in order to purify and resurrect itself. The atheistic moment of Christianity occurs when Jesus speaks upon the cross: *E'li, E'li, la'ma sabachtha'ni* ('my God, my God, why have you forsaken me?') since it is only after uttering this expression of radical doubt that God, through Jesus, resurrects his own belief into universal form. Atheism is therefore permitted, chronologically as a mediator between inadequate belief and resurrected universality. Nestled here, somewhere close to Christianity and yet approaching the position of the Muslims, are the Hindus, whose social bond resembles and accelerates Christian idolatry. It is clear from the Ancient Vedic text 'the *Upinashads*' that subjects are encouraged to find in each and every being around them, and also in oneself, the immanently transcendental being of a God. This is why the greeting 'Namaste' (and its various regional variations) not only demonstrates respect but literally states that subjects 'bow to the divine that exists within you.'

Finally, Islam functions through the foreclosure of the symbolic Father of the law, which returns, subsequently, within the real of the Arabic language itself. Indeed, it is a requirement that one speak Arabic while praying as a Muslim. If English has become today's global language of capitalism, because, in many ways it now exists an auxiliary or alternative language for global business, then Arabic remains a universal language that does not cross-cut the world's linguistic communities but rather seeks in the end to overcome them. I make this claim not as a critique of the Arabic language but rather in empathetic understanding of it: Arabic does not seek to be an 'alternative language,' since, for many Muslims, it is the language of belief itself – it is God's language. English does not pretend to be the language of God, but rather, existing alongside the world's various linguistic communities, it is happy to tolerate them and to incorporate words from this or that community. English is therefore the language of secularism just as capitalism is the political-economic system of alternatives (and this is where Marxists and Anarchists are wrong: capitalism does not require an alternative because it presents itself precisely as the alternative to all of the world's dogmatic political-economic systems; what capitalism requires, therefore, is a dogma). In any case, within the Arabic language (whether Quranic or Modern Arabic) there is a sudden intrusion of phallic signifiers, a certain proliferation of the names of God. There are not only ninety-nine names of God, there are also expressions used by those who do not even consciously claim to belief: 'insha'Allah,' 'alhamdulillah,' 'masha'Allah,' and so on.

Contrary to popular claims: atheism is permitted within Islam, but only as if it were in the past. Thus, the testimony of faith, the shahada (la 'ilaha 'illa llah muhammadun rasulu llah) includes within the first clause the statement of atheism ('there is no God ...') followed by a statement which retroactively determines the conditions of belief ('...but God, ...'). Thus, Islam is a religion of the apres-coup, of the 'afterward.' Not only is the Quran believed to be the last chapter in the Abrahamic trilogy, but it rewrites and rereads everything which came before. This is how we can reconcile the following two Islamic claims: first, that we are hardwired with belief in God; and, second, that we are allowed to be atheist if it was a position prior to our testimony. Since we are already born with belief, it is only from the perspective of the future that are able to claim that we were not. The past is here truly written always from the judgments of the future. Who could not see in the Islamic love of fate a parallel with the Nietzschean axiom of amor fati? Indeed, Nietzsche's love may even be said to be a love of the judgment of the future which defines and governs that which the subject now lives. He writes: 'I want to learn more and more to see as beautiful what is necessary in things. Amor fati: let that be my love henceforth!' (Nietzsche, IV: $276). Nietzsche here demonstrates that the death of god is once again related essentially to the conviction of Christians. Bracketing Nietzsche's position on the death of God, we might transport this love of fate, insha'Allah.

I return again to my thread: the problem with the various responses to the horrific incidents that have been happening against Muslims around the world (e.g, in New Zealand, and also in my previous hometown of Peterborough, Ontario in Canada) is as follows: the ideology of secularism presents an apparent equality or symmetry of terms without properly engaging the differences at the level of discourse. There are two simultaneous problems. First, the ostensibly secular and tolerant position (which insists upon allowing diverse perspectives or voices) is absolutely intolerant toward Islam. Structurally speaking, once again, secularism and tolerance are fundamentally Christian principles (although, it is true, that we can find statements of secularism within Islam too, they are not at the fore). But the problem is also that Islamic religious discourse itself is intolerant of secularism – or, put differently, there is an intolerance toward the principle of tolerance. Zakir Naik provided the following argument:

> Islam is the most secular religion in that we are the most tolerant. But our tolerance is also truthful. Many people feel that tolerance means that you should tolerate belief in any God. What I point out to them is that we need tolerance and truth at the same time. Suppose that one person claims that 2 + 2 = 5, while another claims that 2 +2 = 4. Tolerance does not mean that I can say both are true. True tolerance is to say that 2 + 2 = 4. I don't agree that 2 + 2 = 5. It is my duty as a Muslim to correct the misconception.

Islam presents itself in terms of a universality of belief while secularism presents itself as relativistic regarding belief. For Islamic scholars this implies that there is a universality to truth – and that this universality of truth (not necessarily an objectivity to truth) is nonetheless tolerant toward relative misconceptions or distortions of that truth. Paradoxically, then, true tolerance consists of avoiding the very notion of secular tolerance. Tolerance is a bit like happiness or staring at the sun: if you truly want to see it, you must start by look awry.

3. **Love is Traumatic**

This is why love does not consist essentially of our tolerance of the loved one. There are other modalities of love situated according to religious discourse. Today we should not ask ourselves: 'how can we love our Muslim neighbours?,' and so on, but rather: why is it that whenever we demonstrate love for our Muslim neighbours we end up unknowingly inflicting an altogether more profound epistemic violence upon groups of people by elevating and celebrating the triumph of the Golden Rule? Finally, I would claim that love is today the least of possibilities. Everywhere it meets a startling challenger: the lover is presumed by his colleagues, friends, and family to be sick. He is seen as addicted to that which nonetheless inflicts him with a profound torment, and which, what is terrible for the capitalist worldview, disrupts his career and destabilizes his harmony and well-being. If the old paradigm was responsible for producing lovers who suffered from doubts (e.g., the lover could be heard, if only in a whisper, reflecting upon his doubts about his relationship) then today this paradigm has fallen and given rise to an altogether more troubling and promising possibility: the lover no longer suffers from doubt but rather from certainty. How? When one is certain, the problem is that the Other is not also certain! We see this new form of suffering emerging also in the world of gender theory: whereas once the problem was 'gender trouble,' whereby one did not know which washroom was the correct one, one did not know whether or not one lived up to the ideals of femininity, and so on, then, today, the problem is 'gender certainty.' We see this new form of suffering emerging in the trans* movement whereby the subject sometimes experiences a certainty regarding the reality of their gender but suffers from a society which refuses to recognize that reality (see Rousselle, 2019b). A popular joke retold often by Slavoj Žižek and Alenka Zupančič seems fitting for this new world of love and certainty. A man who believes himself to be a grain of corn rushes to his psychoanalyst: 'help me, I am going to be eaten by a giant chicken!' The psychoanalyst takes on the case and cures him after several months. Years pass, and the man returns: 'help me, help me!' The psychoanalyst, stumped, responds: 'But I thought I cured you: you no longer believe that you are a grain of corn?' The man exclaims: 'I know that, stupid, but the chicken doesn't!' This is the problem of today's lover: he knows very well that he is in love but struggles to convince the chicken of this same fact.

I aim to rescue love from the hegemony that Christian secularism has had over it. I aim to motion from perverse love toward the revolutionary love of certainty. In other words, what I am championing here is a love of delusion rather than a disavowed love of images. We can find remnants of the new paradigm of love already in Islamic teachings, but also in the new teachings of the World Association of Psychoanalysis. My attempt, to put it in a word, is to make love revolutionary in an age which has secured itself against any militant conviction (in favour of fleeting temptations). If only one or two in the future will be armed with this revolutionary commitment of love, then all will not be lost. But, as Lacan reminds us, that will not necessarily constitute progress. Today's lovers will suffer under the pressures of a world that is not and never will be ready for them. They will move fast in love, or else constitute themselves as patient 'Saints' of love: they shall refuse the capitalist dynamics that push them toward another partial solution to subjective destitution. With luck, they will render themselves useless for this world, they will deny professionalization, reject the temptation to mingle with yet another lover, and stand strong in their place despite the overwhelming void that traumatizes them in the core of their being.

II
Certainty

1. Loving Beyond Possessions

I begin with the following claim: love – defined as a 'wish to be loved' (Lacan, 1977: 253) – today confronts two opposing threats: relinquishment and foreclosure. The first threat concerns the relinquishment of love through the giving up of any 'fall' accompanying the union of lovers. To relinquish love is to desire to possess the other or to iron out love's depth by transforming the experience into a consistent and predictable encounter. Though the subject is equipped with the possibility of falling in love, he nonetheless succumbs to the temptation to love without risk, to love without pain, or to love without anxiety. These are the temptations described at length by Slavoj Žižek (2015), Alain Badiou (2012), and Massimo Recalcati (2020). The lover goes on to desire 'happiness' or 'his other half,' the latter of which is only an indication that he desires to be made 'complete' or 'whole' through the technique of his love. The lover therefore gives what he believes himself to have (e.g., money, ability, good looks, charm, knowledge, wisdom, experiences, and so on) to somebody he hopes actually wants it.

There nonetheless persists for him a subtle awareness of the inadequacies of his approach, and, as he ever confronts the limits of the logic of possession and consistency, his emotional life becomes thoroughly permeated by anxiety. This first failure in love is linked to a fundamental deception. It is by losing possession of the loved one as an object that the lover provisionally protects himself from acute feelings which reveal to him the following trauma: he did not truly have the loved one from the very beginning. This makes his feelings of loss intensely charged. It is by losing the loved one as an object and by passing through the concomitant feelings of mourning and sorrow that the subject renews his primordial deception. All the more he tricks himself into believing that at one time he truly possessed her. It is only by going through this emotional turmoil repeatedly that he can convince himself of actually having something to lose. But to *actually* lose somebody or something is to lose the very foundation upon which those feelings of loss could ever be sustained in the first place. Then, the deeper threat to love today is the loss of the ability to lose itself, it is the foreclosure of the very possibility of losing love itself.

There are new lessons that we might gather from the ancient narrative of love in the legend of Orpheus and Eurydice. Orpheus's musical gift, his *lalangue,* was related to his ability to persuade others. Perhaps he once used this gift to entice Eurydice, though she soon became the object cause of another man's desire. Aristaeus, a shepherd, was so captivated by her that he chased her throughout the forest in an attempt to grasp her. Of course, she fled from his hunt, stepped onto a snake, and then died. Now, in sorrow because of his apparent loss, Orpheus turned again to the use of his musical talents in an effort to convince the gods to allow him to retrieve her from the underworld. His *lalangue* was so alluring that all of the objects and beings of the world around him, all of nature itself, were touched by the sweet sounds of his suffering. It becomes clear here that Eurydice, like all of nature itself, becomes implicated in *his* elaborate phantasy: what he desires is to possess her, to produce her as an extension of himself, to procure her as his phallus.

We should recognize in this an important point made by Lacan and his followers: 'woman is a symptom of man' (Lacan, 1975). We should not naively assume that this is some sort of anti-feminist – or, worse, anti-woman – statement. Rather, it implies that man sees in the woman not only the cause of his desire but also the possibility for a fleeting concealment of his foundational and persisting trauma. Woman becomes for him the phallic substitute for his castration anxiety. Pierre-Gilles Gueguen explained it as follows:

> A woman turns herself into a symptom for a man as she incarnates for the man the phallus that the mother lacks and which for the man denies maternal castration. Thus, a woman serves as a screen in man's relation to castration, and that is why she is a symptom. (Gueguen, 2010)

The woman is a symptom for man, from the perspective of man, because she functions as a love object which quells the unbearable anxiety of castration and lack. We should not simply presume that woman 'plugs up' the lack since this would imply that she produces in man a general foreclosure of desire, that is, psychosis. It is more accurate to claim that she produces in him the very possibility of lack even while she introduces an unbearable make-shift solution to the anxiety arising therefrom. Does this not explain why men in 1990's television sitcoms would exclaim: 'Women: you can't live with them, you can't live without them!' This, precisely, is the definition of a symptom: something you can't live with or without, a problem which was produced through our very attempt to solve another underlying problem. The problem, of course, is that the underlying problem is a *necessary* problem while the symptomatic problem is rather *pathological*. The aim of psychoanalysis is often to identify with the necessary symptom of castration anxiety and to overcome the pathological symptom.

The legend of Orpheus and Eurydice demonstrates very well how man's phallic gaze denies the lack in the maternal Other. When Orpheus moved the world with his beautiful sorrow, he also subjected that world to the masculine process of phantasy laid out by Lacan in his graph of *sexuation* (presented on March 13, 1973). Love can only exist for Orpheus by keeping Eurydice within his sight, and it is threatened by relinquishment the moment she disappears or dies. Her fall into the underworld could have been the impetus for a purer form of love which possibly endures beyond the fall, and yet it was the moment of his return to a dialectic of trauma and desperation. The urgency of his plea demonstrates also the truth of his trauma. Bernard Seynhaeve wrote in his argument for the 17th Congress of the New Lacanian School that '[t]his "urgency" is the traumatic moment when, for a subject, the signifying chain [consistency, image, ego, body] has been broken' (Seynhaeve, 2019). Orpheus responds through urgency, thereby reducing the love encounter to a moment of haste: rather than retroactively determining the conditions of love within the trauma of their disunion, he erroneously traces it through the logic of possession, consistency, visibility, and communicability.

Let us presume that Orpheus's plea was an urgent demand made as an appeal to the Gods. In response, he received the following proviso: 'go to the underworld and retrieve her, but be patient, do not look back at her until you have left the underworld (otherwise you will lose her for all of eternity).' We might claim that this was an attempt on behalf of the gods to introduce the cure of time, namely patience, to Orpheus (who so required it). Was this proviso not itself an attempt to thwart the urgent demand? Seynhaeve claims that there is an urgent push toward truth at the level of the drive, and yet this truth can never be captured by the signifier. Orpheus's holophrastic music, his *lalangue,* pushed him toward certainty – but it was a certainty coupled by the urgency of his demand to once again possess Eurydice. Seynhaeve writes that 'there is always urgency, there is always something that pushes, that urges, that presses and that is beyond transference, even if one takes one's time or lets it drag on. […] We run after the truth, says Lacan; […] but truth cannot be caught by the signifier' (Seynhaeve, 2019). The patience of time, what I am tempted to qualify using the neologism *passience* – a coupling of patience, passion, and jouissance – introduces distance from an urgency of the drives, outside of signification.

There was within the underworld of Orpheus's passion, before making his final exit with Eurydice on hand, a moment during which he perceived a deception on behalf of the gods. Indeed, he believed for that moment that he was the victim of an elaborate trick: it was not truly her who followed him, but rather a ghost – a semblance. At this point we should be willing to risk a radical interpretation: it was not, as we often presume, in this moment of haste, when he looked back to verify her presence, that he lost her forever. Rather, we should accept from the beginning that she was never there *except as semblance*. He thus witnessed the truth: the truth is that which slips away from our grasp. It is by insisting that he suddenly lost her that he renewed the fundamental phantasy of the woman's existence (or, to put it in our previous terms, he exchanged necessity for pathology). Lacan taught us that 'the woman does not exist' (Lacan, 1999: 16), and this was as unsettling a truth as one could possibly imagine. Is it not the case that the gods were here revealing this startling truth to Orpheus? They demonstrated that which Orpheus was still not willing to accept: that love exists always in some relationship to an incomprehensible and foundational moment of loss. Indeed, this was a truth that the shepherd was better prepared to accept than Orpheus.

We can see some evidence that this argument was also made in antiquity. For example, Phaedrus, in Plato's Symposium, made use of numerous examples to bolster his argument that love is intimately connected with loss. Although Alcestis was willing to die for her husband, it is not true that Orpheus had the same courage for Eurydice. In fact, Phaedrus implied that Orpheus exhibited cowardly love while Eurydice had courageous love. Orpheus descended into the underworld without courageously passing through his own death, and this resulted in the feeling that he lost something he once possessed, Eurydice. Ancient Greek philosophy therefore demonstrates – before any of the later adaptations – that not only did the Gods intend to deceive Orpheus, in order to show him the truth, but that Orpheus, as a coward, was up against a woman who, as is often the case in love, was much more courageous and virtuous than he. Isn't this also how we should read the story of the Prophet of Islam when he discovered the angel Gabriel? Shocked by the first revelation, he raced home, often stumbling, until he approached his wife Khadijah. Khadijah reassured and offered confirmation of his visions in two ways: first, with her response: 'God is witness, he has not sent you this Word that you should fail and prove unworthy

29

and that He should then give you up. How can God do such a thing, while you are kind and considerate to your relations, help the poor and the forlorn and bear their burdens?,' and, second, by obtaining confirmation from her cousin, Waraqa bin Naufal.

Orpheus chased Eurydice and retrieved her from the underworld only to convince himself that he never lost her in the first place. The claim that I am trying to make is not at all the following banal and popular one: that love cannot exist without the fall into the underworld. I am also not trying to claim that love can only exist if one is willing and prepared to risk a fall into the underworld. Finally, I do not intend to make the claim that one should be wary of the temptation to conflate gaze/image and love. All of these positions lead us closer to the truth, but they do not bring us all the way. My claim is much more radical, since to love is not the triumph against a fall into the world: love exists as the very truth of the fall itself, since what is most fallen in love is the possibility of love itself. In other words, love is not what results from a fall and it is not the possibility of fall, neither is it the rejection of the gaze: love is itself there within the fall. I would add only that in love there is an extra ingredient: an attitude of fidelity and courage *vis-à-vis* this fall, which insists upon moving through, accepting, and sharing the primordial trauma. And the only way this may be done is by disrupting the subjective urgency of the demand by allowing it to persist and to therefore endure in time.

This is also a lesson we could take from the recent debates regarding the wearing of a scarf by Muslim women (and also non-Muslims) outside of Islamic cultures. Indeed, the debates have been particularly fierce in French secular societies such as France and the Canadian French-speaking province of Quebec. Is it not the case that the foreclosure of the scarf by secular extremists only renews a culture which privileges the urgency of the phallic gaze so as to symptomatically 'make women exist?' The rejection of the scarf is in an attempt to renew the pathological deception that women actually exist by re-inscribing her within the phallic gaze (and thereby reducing her once again to her visibility). We should read closely the Quran on this question. Surah Al-Ahzab reads as follows: '[a]nd when you ask [your wives] for something, ask them from behind a partition [curtain]. That is purer for your hearts and their hearts' (33:53; my translation). Perhaps the correct way to read this is not as a moral axiom – as both fanatic literalists and fanatic secularists read it – but rather as an ontological statement: one cannot possess woman through the phallic gaze because all authentic relationships with woman require man to pass through the paradoxical acceptance of *not-having*, of what Lacan calls 'minus-phi' or 'minus-the-phallus.' Once again, god reveals the heart only through a curtain or image. This is a lesson Christians are less willing to since for them often – but not always – the function of the image is not to conceal but rather to conceal the fact of there being nothing to conceal.

Slavoj Žižek and Alenka Zupančič (2017) have discussed the role of the 'fig leaves' in the early account of Adam in the garden. Genesis 3:7 reads: '[t]hen the eyes of both of them were opened, and they realized they were naked; so they sewed fig leaves together and made coverings for themselves.' There were debates concerning the illustration of 'belly buttons' in early biblical paintings. If Adam has a 'belly button' then does it not imply that he was biologically born to a biological father who preceded him? The debates were resolved by simply extending the fig leaf from the genitals toward the belly button. Yet, there within Islam, already an answer to this riddle has existed: the Quran is very clear that God does not have any sons biologically, he is not a *biological* father; he can only be understood as a 'metaphorical' father. Thus, the father, metaphorically, operates as a metaphor, and not, principally, as person who is anything like our own fathers (who are fallible). For example, in Surah al-Badarah (2:116) there is a rectification against the misleading Christian belief: since God is understood as beyond gender, and since father indicates a that God is 'male'; the Quran states clearly that God is not a 'man.' This challenges Christian belief itself since all of the prophets were referred to as 'the son of God.' The only way out for Christians is to presume that 'son of' indicates a metaphorical process rather than a strict biological one. In its purest form, an image functions as a partition or cover which conceals the fact of there being nothing at all to conceal.

This is the true function of an image. An image does not stand in the way of truth by covering over the real or filling it in. It stands in the way of truth by offering itself as the only truth: by concealing the fact of there being nothing that can be concealed in the first place. The curtain of man's phantasy shrouds woman in deceptive ways. Woman's clothing is therefore an extension of man's innate phantasies; we might repurpose Marshall McLuhan's theses about the extensions of man by claiming that woman's clothing is a symptomatic extension of man's phantasy: her skin. It is an extension of her visibility. It is not that this spiritual phantasmatic dimension somehow exists independent of the material reality. It is not as if man could just avoid the phantasy of woman's existence and therefore return to some more primordial and real encounter. This is perhaps another way to read Hegel's controversial claim that 'the spirit is a bone,' since, within spiritual traditions phantasy is precisely what is most real about reality. The curtain of man's phantasy shrouds woman in deceptive projections of beautification, thereby rendering her inexistent, and yet, at the same time, this is nonetheless what is most truthful about man and woman.

We do not know who invented clothing, but we can be sure that it was first invented by men. Indeed, the old testament – important for all Abrahamic religions – teaches us that the first woman was clothed by flesh itself after being made from the first man's rib. The King James translation reads: 'this is the bone of my bones, and flesh of my flesh: she shall be called Woman because she was taken out of Man.' The awareness of flesh as curtain or partition is what is most at stake in any relationship with woman, so much so that, in love, we cannot get beyond it. Once again we should repurpose Marshall McLuhan's theses of the extensions of man: it is not only that clothing is the extension of skin, but also, rather, that skin is revealed as the first clothing. When we claim that the spirit is a bone, we also mean to suggest that man cannot but fall in love with woman as his phantasy, he cannot but dress her up via his phallic rib/bone. In other words, we cannot but find within the relationship to woman a certain trauma since there is no way to authentically access her outside of the phallic orbit without succumbing to this trauma. Islam, more than the other Abrahamic faiths, seems to prepare its followers to engage with this trauma: through the various partitions, curtains, regulations, and so on, there is an affirmation of woman's non-existence which paradoxically only reveals her and liberates her from the phallic orbit.

Perhaps the most contentious technique for revealing woman as inexistent is by way of the hijab, niqab, or burka. The obstacle of the curtain actively constructs (rather than negates) the sexual relationship. Women are therefore not simply concealed and oppressed within Islamic culture; indeed, those feminists who proclaim that the scarf is an instrument of oppression miss an important point. It is by removing the partition that the real trauma occurs. If woman were exposed as radically inexistent, we confront a level of anxiety that is perhaps too much for Western men to bear. The American neo-liberal obsession with 'free choice,' 'free speech,' and 'control of one's own body,' unfortunately misses the fundamental deception of the unconscious: it is precisely when one believes oneself to be free that one even more finds oneself determined by symbolic and real forces that urgently push us into a symptomatic whirlwind. It is by asserting the existence of 'the woman' as an authentic identity and object of love that she becomes more easily objectified, possessed, and rendered more consistent with capitalist-patriarchal society. It is only by disrupting the phallic gaze by way of exposing the curtain itself that the fundamental trauma which gives rise to patriarchal society can be explored. This is precisely what the scarf does: it reveals woman for what she effectively is: a silhouette, who, because of her non-existence, exists all the more dynamically within the imaginary.

A common assumption is that Western secular societies are therefore more sexually permissive and therefore more lustful than various Islamic cultures. Yet, is it not precisely through the awareness of the curtain of one's phantasy that one can paradoxically grasp woman even more and therefore eroticize the sexual relationship? Despite claims made by popular discourse, Islam is among the most sexually progressive of the world's religions. Abu Dharr once claimed that the prophet stated: '[i]n sexual intercourse for any one of you there is a reward.' Some replied to him with a question: 'when any one of us fulfils his desire, will he have a reward?' The prophet replied: 'Do you not see that if he were to do it in a haram [sinful] manner, he would be punished for that? So, if he does it in a halal manner, he will be rewarded.' Indeed, some claim that Islam makes sexual pleasure an obligation between husbands and wives while nonetheless affirming a certain fidelity in love which endures beyond and despite the trauma – precisely as a push of the trauma itself.

2. Sharing Suffering

The problem for Orpheus was that he insisted upon the removal of the curtain/obstacle in order to return to the image/face of Eurydice. He also did not realize that there is an intimate connection of love with primordial suffering. Thus, the goal is not to look beyond the image/face of the loved one in order to arrive at a more authentic underlying reality but rather to find what within the image/face is already a response to a primordial trauma. Love is the name we might use for the transmission and sharing of a space of suffering/loss precisely through the curtain, partition, or image. Or, in other words, love requires an aesthetics of suffering. Bracha L. Ettinger has developed her entire post-Lacanian theory around this basic idea. She wrote:

> [There exists] a deep capacity to join in love and in suffering, in sorrow and in joy, in compassion. Freud talked on the affect and effect of [...] uncanny anxiety. I argue that human affects like compassion and awe are just as uncanny and as primary as this anxiety. (Ettinger, 2017)

Ettinger was here discussing not just the anxiety of lack or castration but also and more essentially the traumatic anxiety of compassion, the latter of which is no doubt more foundational than castration anxiety. Since passion implies endurance through suffering, and not, as the contemporary naïve interpretation puts it 'joy' or 'happiness,' and the prefix com- adds to this a zone of paradoxical union. Within Lacanian psychoanalysis this primordial substratum of enjoyable suffering is referred to as jouissance. Love is therefore not isolated from suffering but is that which necessitates or pushes the subject toward some delusional certainty; indeed, it pushes the subject toward his own invention as subject. This is its *passience:* the endurance of jouissance through the beauty of an unshakable conviction. Thus, the 'Passion of the Christ,' or the other 'passion narratives,' document not 'happiness' or 'joy' – it is not that Christ was pursuing his love of a skilled trade or hobby – but rather suffering as the outcome of a fundamental and unshakable religious conviction.

My claim is that delusional certainty in love can offer the traumatized subject – or, put another way, the psychotic subject – a mode of stabilization. Love is indeed among the healthiest of delusions for subjects who increasingly report traumas to their psychoanalysts. Whereas the traditional subject suffered from doubt within the 'prison-house of language,' by being torn from either end by signifiers (since the subject is 'represented [to a signifier] for another signifier'; Lacan, 1977b: 207), today's subjects suffer not from doubt but rather from certainty. Subjects today suffer from the loss of this very subjective space within the symbolic. The symbolic exists rather as a frightening apparition within the real. The old subject of doubt forever questioned his love relationship (e.g., 'is she the right woman for me?,' 'is marriage a prison?'), but today's subject asks a question in relation to certainty (e.g., 'she is definitely not the right person for me' or 'she is perfect!'). Today's subject of love seems torn not between signifiers as an expression of love but rather in oscillation between one of two positions: 'if I have any doubt about her, then she isn't the right one' and/or 'I have no doubts about it, she is the one for me!'

The subjective suffering by way of certainty causes problems at the level of the Other: today's subjects are certain, and their problem is that the Other is not certain too (see Rousselle, 2019). On the one hand, this seems like a fundamental displacement of responsibility. For example, the old joke about the man who visited in psychoanalyst because he thought he was a grain of corn about to be eaten by a giant chicken demonstrates the fact that his cure missed the following displacement, 'I know I am no longer a grain of corn, but the chicken doesn't know it!' Yet, things are much more troubling here. The traumatized subject requires not this simple level of displacement but rather a more delicate procedure of bringing the Other into existence narcissistically precisely through the subject's own certainty. It is not that the chicken doesn't know it but rather that the chicken does not yet exist for the subject and so, through the chicken's uncertainty or lack of knowledge, he must be brought into existence as a semblance. This shift from problems of doubt toward problems of certainty can be demonstrated in the world of gender theory. If gender anxiety was once defined by the gendered subject as an uncertainty over his or her gender identity (e.g., 'what does it mean to be a woman?'), and this, precisely, is what caused 'gender trouble,' then today the situation of trans* people demonstrates another modality of suffering: 'I am certain about my gender identity but other people are not certain about it, and this is my fundamental problem' (this thesis is developed at length in Rousselle, 2019b).

One way to read Bracha L. Ettinger's post-Lacanian 'matrixial' theory is to claim that it is possible to share the delusion of one's certainty in love despite an inadequacy in paternal or phallic signification. When the foundation for love has been eradicated, all that remains is for the increase in the scope of one's certainty. Thus, against Alain Badiou's claim that 'love is communism for two' (Badiou, 2012), I would claim that love is also the sharing of delusional certainty against the trauma of the real. This is why Ettinger's interpretation of the Orpheus/Eurydice legend is a nice corrective to the interpretations propounded by popular culture (such as in the film *Black Orpheus*). Ettinger places Eurydice within the phallic gaze of the masculine subject. Judith Butler summarizes Ettinger's position:

> Eurydice is, as we know, already lost, already gone, already dead, and yet, at the moment in which our gaze apprehends her, she is there, there for the instant in which she is there. And the gaze by which she is apprehended is the gaze

through which she is banished. Our gaze pushes her back to death, since we are prohibited from looking, and we know that by looking, we will lose her. And we will not lose her for the first time, but we will lose her again, and it will be by virtue of our own gaze that she will be lost to us, and that she will, as a result, be apprehensible only *as* loss. So, it is not just that she is lost, and we discover her again to be lost, but that in the very act of seeing, we lose. (Butler, 2004: 95-6)

This lesson of Eurydice is also the hidden truth revealed in plain sight within the fundamental message of Christianity. Whereas Judaism finds an image/body ascending in the figure of Moses (the 'at-least-one' to have the courage to *ascend* the mountain), Christianity locates an image/body in the figure of Jesus who, through God's own humiliation, *descends* from heaven down into the human underworld. Through *ascension*, the image of man connects with the symbolic God as revealed via the tablets of the law (thus, there is a rejection of the image in favor of God's prohibitions). But through *descension,* the Symbolic God connects with the image of man as revealed in the figure of Christ himself. Thus, there is a disavowal of the symbolic God through the worship of Christ. This couple of Symbolic-Imaginary and Imaginary-Symbolic form the basis of the Judeo-Christian legacy and each in their own way form a defence against the primordial trauma of the real. They safeguard against the possibility of psychosis by introducing neurotic or perverse possibilities.

The message of love in Christianity is therefore that God distanced himself from himself through the image of Jesus. Jesus is therefore not an essentially symbolic name but is rather essentially an image, body, or consistency. Slavoj Žižek wrote:

God himself, the universal Substance, has to 'humiliate' himself, to fall into his own creation, 'objectivize' himself, to appear as a singular miserable human individual, in all its abjection, i.e., abandoned by God. The distance of man from God is thus the distance of God from himself. (Žižek, 2012: 169)

It is in this precise sense that love consists of an ontological gap within one's own being. Christian love is not essentially about having or possessing an object, and neither is it about the image covering over a fundamental 'being' which must be exposed in its raw material form. Rather, Christianity demonstrates that man, like God, is fundamentally incomplete, that he embodies more than anything else what Lacan called a 'lack-of-being.' Christianity gives body to something in this world that has already fallen, that has already experienced a certain trauma, by gradually increasing the scope of that body so as to allow it to endure in time via the holy spirit (e.g., the holy spirit is another name for community of believers). We might claim that the holy spirit occurs as a consequence of Jesus's militant and delusional conviction and by those who are prepared to love with certainty against the trauma of being itself. Christian love shares its lack-of-being through the body of Christ and through a necessity and acceptance of God's primordial public/scopic humiliation. The movement from Judaism toward Christianity is therefore also a movement from the symbolic's triumph over the inadequacy of the image/idol toward one which discovers the triumph of the symbolic's inadequacy via the endurance of an image.

Thus, the truth of Jesus, which is the revelation of divinity, occurs not only after Jesus experiences epistemological doubt while upon the cross ('My God, My God, why have you forsaken me?') but also and more fundamentally when the body of Jesus was placed inside of a tomb. It was when placed in the tomb that he vanished; thus, truth was revealed, once again, by the Gods through the disappearances or subtraction of the visible and sensible. This was also Rhiannon Graybill's position in a wonderful essay titled 'Caves of the Hebrew Bible: A Speleology' (Graybill, 2018). Graybill writes that 'Biblical caves [are] associated with concealment, providing a hiding place for people and taboo practices and things. [...] [And] they are significant to the analysis of gender' (ibid., 1). She continues,

[t]he cave is a symbolic passage between worlds, from heaven to earth or from earth to the underworld. It is a place of birth and

death, at onc e a womb and a tomb. The cave conceals, covers, and contains; it also reveals, uncovers, and unearths. (ibid., 1-2)

Why shouldn't we presume that the cave is the place not of the simple Platonic topology whereby there is an outside and an inside, but rather as a Klein bottle: the place where God himself turns in upon himself in order to give birth to something else, the place where death intrudes into life, and the place where transcendence emerges from immanent processes. The connection with gender is interesting here: we should propose also that woman is to man what is most symptomatic and truthful about him: that he is a creature with the possibility of loving another as himself.

In any case, St. Ignatius of Loyola was probably deceived when he instructed his fellow Christians, the Jesuits, to produce their own 'lack-of-being' through the following spiritual exercises:

[C]hastise the flesh, that is, giving it sensible pain, which is given by wearing haircloth or cords or iron chains next to the flesh, by scourging or wounding oneself, and by other kinds of austerity. [...] What appears most suitable and most secure with regard to penance is that the pain should be sensible in the flesh and not enter within the bones, so that it give pain and not illness. For this it appears to be more suitable to scourge oneself with thin cords, which give pain exteriorly, rather than in another way which would cause notable illness within. (St. Ignatius of Loyola, 1914: 32)

Slavoj Žižek (2003) has claimed that Christianity is perverse at its core in that it operates according to a clinical logic of 'disavowal':

[P]erversion is a double strategy to counteract [God's] nonexistence: an (ultimately deeply conservative, nostalgic attempt to install the law artificially [...] and, in a complementary way, a no less desperate attempt to codify the very transgression of the Law. In the perverse reading of Christianity, God first threw humanity into Sin in order to create the opportunity for saving it through Christ's sacrifice. (Zizek, 2003)

But this characterization misses a crucial point. St. Ignatius could not have known that this masochistic gesture only demonstrates that the subject enjoys too much his various productions of suffering; he could not have known that the infliction of loss and trauma upon the body is only a strategy to avoid the acceptance of primordial loss. Put another way, if the loss was not yet produced for the subject, then what becomes forsaken in the production of loss is loss itself. Any effort to produce the lost loss only further deceives the Christian subject into false belief that there was already something to lose. Thus, the Jesuits presume that the body pre-exists its trauma, when, it seems to me that it is rather a beautiful consequence of trauma. Does the sacrifice of Jesus not demonstrate that he only truly lives on when he does so outside of the phallic worship of his image? The secret of Christian love – one not accepted by many Christians – is found in the urgency of 'death drive.' Jesus, in the King James Bible, says: '[m]ost assuredly, I say unto you, unless a grain of wheat falls into the ground and dies, it remains alone; but if it dies, it produces much grain' (John 12-17). We could interpret this as the necessity of death for pushing the subject to endure as a certainty in life.

The problem of the Jesuits is that they give themselves the impression of 'having' by pounding away and removing the body's flesh. This misses Christ's essential lesson: his body was not there from the beginning, it was given form through the certainty of his community of believers: '[f]or when two or three [are] gathered in my name, there I am with them' (Matthew 18:20). He does not pre-exist the two or three but is retroactively created as a certainty through the cut of any two; Christ knew perfectly well that the presumption of a pre-existing body, a 'one,' prematurely sutures the field of spiritual thinking. This was also the point made in the 1950s by Lacan's most faithful disciples, Jacques-Alain Miller, Yves Duroux, and others, when they began to work forward on their theory of 'suture.' This work focused on a strange cocktail of Lacanian insights into Gottleb Frege's *Foundations of Arithmetic* in order to demonstrate that the 'one' is only possible by first positing two. Put another way, every 'one' has within itself already a fundamental scission, as

Alain Badiou has put it, and this scission exposes the body to its real dimension of 'cut.' Yet, paradoxically, this 'cut' is also what gives rise to the body of Christ. Therefore, those who follow St. Ignatius of Loyola on this point deceptively decide to affirm a logic of 'having' the 'one' through the removal of the body: but the body is something we 'have' only in the sense of a 'hole' or 'void' which can never be sutured. As one Lacanian put it: '[we] have a body, but a body inscribed with trauma outside of meaning, a hole at the center of being which is surrounded by an image, and with this image, he makes a world' (Adler, 2018). Whether Orpheus or the Jesuits, the spiritual practices are similar: the production of a loss in order to convince oneself of 'having.'

Jacques-Alain Miller demonstrates, by way of the Lacanian notion of 'lack' (roughly equivalent to 'not-having'), one of many modalities of love at our disposal:

> [T]o love is to recognize your lack and give it to the other, place it in the other. It's not giving what you possess, goods and presents, it's giving something else that you don't possess, which goes beyond you. To do that you have to assume your lack, your 'castration' as Freud used to say. And that is essentially feminine. One only really loves from a feminine position. Love feminises. That's why love is always a bit comical in a man. (Miller, 2013)

We should be particularly attentive to the words used by Miller. Giving one's lack is no more a call to sadism (e.g., striking the flesh as they do in certain Shia sects or in the Jesuit order) than it is a call to masochism (e.g., producing anxiety or lack in the Other). Accepting responsibility for one's lack, as well as for the lack in the Other, is not at all the same as producing a lack which is lacking. This is why Miller claimed that one has to 'assume your lack,' since he presumes that the lack has already been installed (and not that the subject has opted for the psychotic solution whereby 'lack itself is lacking'). Though Christianity demonstrates that love consists of various techniques of humiliation and degradation of the subject – revealing an underlying femininity – this is not in of itself a reason to presume that it is inherently perverse. My attempt is to rescue

41

Christianity from the perverse reading and to subject it to an Islamic reading, or, put differently, my attempt is to find within Christianity the zero-level psychotic moment whereby lack was installed as a perverse solution within psychotic structure.

In the final instance, Christian love interrupts the phantasmatic support of masculine subjectivity by revealing the inherent and a priori destitution of the subject upon which any object-relation or object-possession might occur. In a sense, then, Jesus did not die for our sins but rather he revealed that he was already dead and that he could only be accessed through the intermediary of the image and the body. Put another way, the word sin, which is revealed in the Hebrew as *hata* or in the Greek is related to an error or a missing of the mark, such that the death for sins is rather the convergence of two errors which are universal and primordial. At the same time, there is in Christian love the perverse operation of disavowal with respect to love. There is the following key difference between the meta-ethical cornerstones of Christianity and Islam: Christianity often resurrects its status as a universal discourse by way of the second golden rule to 'love thy neighbour as thyself' (this is a love of difference in order to secure the universal phantasy), thereby revealing a certain logic of disavowal (e.g., 'we respect differences and yet at the same time we wish to offer the one and only truth concerning love'), and Islam often proclaims with certainty that love exists not essentially by respecting differences but rather by coming to common terms with the other religions of the book (e.g., an ethical maxim from the third surah, ayah 64). From a meta-ethical standpoint, then, Christianity does indeed offer the perverse solution for the problem of universality while Islam offers a solution of commonality via the certainty of belief. Islam reveals itself as more aligned with the contemporary structure of subjectivity.

Certainty of belief is secured in Islam precisely by removing from within itself any atheism or non-belief. This removal of the primordial error is akin to the foreclosure of lack. Yet, the problem of the lack-of-belief is central to the three Abrahamic religions, and each, in their own way, has to contend with it even while depending upon it, essentially, for the establishment of their religious doctrine. For example, chronologically speaking, Judaism permits atheism after the symbolic God of the tablet substitutes itself for imaginary idolatry: one can be an atheist after one has already been a Jew. For example, there is the story of Peter Lipton who was '[a] self-confessed "religious atheist," [who was] fully engaged with his religious culture, taking his family to synagogue on Saturdays and teaching children at the Sabbath school. He did not think it was necessary to believe in God to recognize the value of religion in providing the individual with a moral compass' (Rabbi Dow Marmur, 2018). However, for Christians, atheism or non-belief is inscribed precisely within the middle of the discourse's chronology: there is, within the believer's heart, a moment of the fall into the 'dark night of the soul,' so that, finally, a resurrected belief might occur. Descartes' radical doubt exists, like Christ's doubt upon the cross, precisely as a stage in the movement of spiritual renewal and reinvigoration. Thus, Žižek and others (e.g., G. K. Chesterton) have argued that there is a moment within the Christian narrative where God himself – through Jesus – becomes an atheist.

Where does Islam stand on the problem of atheism and non-belief? We often here that Atheism is blasphemous within Islam and that it results in death. Yet, we should be very clear: atheism is considered impossible within Islam because we are all already hardwired with belief, thus, it is impossible to be truly atheist. One might be atheist at the conscious level without recognizing the symbolic determinations of God at the unconscious level. Thus, I repeat Max Stirner's curious passage to Ludwig Feuerbach's humanism: 'our atheists are the most pious people!' They don't know what they know all too well, they don't believe at all what they believe! In any case, there is within Islam the following curious contradiction: on the one hand, one is permitted to be an atheist, chronologically speaking, before one has become a Muslim; yet, on the other hand, there is the claim that one is already born hard-wired with belief; this is why Muslims prefer to use the word 'revert' rather than 'convert.' How are we to reconcile these two ostensibly contradictory claims?

We have here an example of the Hegelian logic of 'positing the presuppositions,' whereby our past belief is installed as *always already there* from the perspective of the future – and, as it were, we cannot do otherwise than to claim that we have always believed but that we have strayed from that belief (e.g., moved away from the 'straight path'). This is demonstrated most obviously in the Islamic emphasis on 'judgment day' (*Yawm ad-Din*) since, as Slavoj Žižek (via Hegel) has argued: 'essence posits its own presuppositions' (Žižek, 2008: 260). Since, at the end of life, according to Muslims, there is a day of judgment, does this not imply that at the end there shall be belief which shall retroactively assume a detraction from inherent belief since the beginning? Indeed, this love of fate, or, retroactive determinations of faith, as an element of a technique messianism, is installed already at the level of casual Arabic language in the expression 'Insha'Allah.' The idea of leaving everything to God's will implies that the future will determine the past, and not, as we might expect, that we resign ourselves to our futures and can therefore just await the coming judgment. It is often supplemented with the following Arabic idiom: 'put your faith in God but always tie your camel.' This means that we are nonetheless responsible for the determinations which will retroactively constitute our faith. Incidentally, this implies that we are *even more* responsible than those who naively believe in 'free will.' Those who naively believe in free will take responsibility only to discredit it in others: if I am free to produce my own destiny then the other, who does not come out so well in the end, must be responsible for his horrible judgment. Islam demonstrates that 'free will' produces an unknowing determination so that we do not know what determines us: we believe ourselves to be free but we are not at all acting freely. Islam moves in an altogether different direction: we align ourselves with the straight path of the divine determinations which compel us, and the difficulty is to *not act as though we are free*. And this is the most difficult responsibility that a human can work through today: to not stray into the crooked path of an ideology of freedom.

It is in Islam that we find movements of certainty in

belief that occur not as a defence against the real but rather as its extension into a body of truth. Whereas Judaism offers a symbolic God of the tablets (installing the prohibitions that we have come to associate with the Lacanian name-of-the-father), Christianity offers an imaginary God of the body; finally, Islam offers a real God whose 'extimacy' is described very well in Surah Qaf (50:16): 'And we have already created man and know what his soul whispers to him, and We are closer to him than his jugular vein.' This is a God who absolutely resists the image and so pushes toward a logic of *sinthome*. Whereas the sinthome – unlike the 'symptom' – is a jouissance which calls out to nobody, likewise within Islam there is nothing which God demands from us, and yet, at the same time, we cannot help but always be in touch with God. Within Islam we find the only religion which fully demonstrates God's unique mode of jouissance: thus, one has only to identify with this radical void of God's enjoyment, with the void which pushes the subject and compels him not toward the image of the body (since, as we know, the exemplary case of 'sinthomatic solutions' was James Joyce who refused imaginary coping techniques) but rather toward a singular mode of organization: writing. Indeed, Surah Al-Qalam (68:1 & 68:2) reads: 'By the pen and what they inscribe; you are not, by the favor of your Lord, a madman.' At the moment of writing we are able to organize God's jouissance and to therefore find within ourselves a mode of jouissance organization.

There is some truth, then, to the popular wisdom that love should never be conflated with any imaginary sense of ownership. When the loved one is reduced to an object, she becomes a mere prop within the domain of man's phantasy. Since the *modus operandi* of the ego is 'possession' and 'consistency,' the love of ownership via the phallic gaze is always ego-love. Wherever this love prevails there is evidence of the axiom that 'it is one's own ego that one loves in love' (Lacan, 1988: 142). This logic was explored most forcefully in Lacan's 19th seminar *Encore,* where the masculine subject is 'sexuated' (castrated) by a phallic signifier. Subsequently, his only recourse is to relate to the object cause of his desire, the woman, as semblance via the phantasmatic circuit.

Yet, any ostensibly possessed object also inadequately conceals the fact of subjective destitution. Indeed, this is one way to interpret the famous Lacanian 'matheme of phantasy' ($<>a): the castrated subject, $, engages with the object cause of his desire through the axis of his own phantasy. However, does this moment of sexuation not align itself most clearly with the Judeo-Christian legacy? The Islamic legacy aligns itself most clearly with the time of the not-all: in some sense, the discourse of Islam does not impart as its truth castration anxiety but rather the installation of oneself as *objet petit a;* there does not exist a single Muslim subject who is not submitted to this anxiety and who therefore contributes to the shared body of Islamic doctrine, the Sunnah.

Masculine love always has this phantasmatic trajectory because love is what makes up for the lack of having itself. Yet, we should not be naïve in presuming that we can escape this logic. We could read this statement on love in relation to the sexual: love is what makes up for the lack of a sexual relationship, but sex should not be read literally as physical copulation or as the union of two beings brought together into one. Quite the opposite: love is nothing more than the name we give to the phantasy of union through sexual copulation. Sex refers to primordial ontological incompleteness, or, in other words, the lack-of-being as well as the lack-of-the-Other. Sex is the hole that exists within any knowledge, within any pattern or consistency, and within any logic of having or possession. Put differently, sex is that which interrupts and intervenes as an obstacle to meaning itself (Zupančič, 2012). Alenka Zupančič writes:

> [S]ex is above all a concept that formulates a persisting contradiction of reality. And [...] this contradiction is involved in the very structuring of [...] being. In this sense, sex is of ontological significance: not as an ultimate reality, but as an inherent twist, or stumbling block, of reality. (Zupančič, 2017: 3)

Sex is the real ontological stratum which remains forever inexpressible within language and image. Sex is the problem for which love offers a potential solution, and yet, at the same time, love is founded upon the ontological rupture of sex. This is why Lacan was able to claim that love is 'outside-sex' (*horsexe*), since it provides the distance through which one might tolerate the profound anxiety of the lack of a sexual relationship. The Lacanian corrective is best expressed in the following way: 'one cannot love except by becoming a non-*haver*, even if one *has* (Lacan, 2015). To love is to give what you do not have, since to locate oneself where one already is, within the real of sex – within the fundamental impossibility of a direct and unmediated relationship – is also to articulate an affirmative love. Lacan was intensely suspicious of love and hate (the two are intertwined in terms of libidinal investments into object-relations) but he nonetheless opened up a space for affirmative love.

We can now discern two fundamental positions on love from Lacan: first, love is to give what one doesn't have (… to somebody who doesn't want it), and; second, love is what makes up for the lack of a sexual relationship. The first axiom is often associated with the earlier Lacanian teachings of the 1950s-1960s while the second is associated with the 'late Lacan' period of the 1970s. Lacan's position on love did not change, rather, new clinical realities most likely emerged: whereas the former seems to affirm a courageous style of love, the latter cautions against love's symptomatic dimension. Indeed, to be a 'non-haver' in love seems to be a courageous attitude against the temptation of love's relinquishment, and to love as a way of compensating for lack seem cowardly *vis-à-vis* the hole of sex. However, is it not possible to also turn these positions around: to be a 'non-haver' in love is all the more to conceal the hole of sex (via the nothing) and to love so as to make up for lack is also courageously to love in spite of the primordial trauma of sex. Once again the Klein bottle can give us an orientation: just as sex is related to the lack-in-being so too love is related to the imaginary substitution of this lack of being; yet, if we move the other way in the Klein bottle, then love can also bring us to the lack-in-being and produce the possibility of an impossible and unsatisfiable sexuality. This impossible sexuality is important for the proliferation of desire, and yet, today, when sexual union seems the easiest of possibilities for most of the neoliberal world, only love can reintroduce it as an obstacle. Courtly love is no longer a deception aimed at making sex appear possible precisely by making it impossible by will, it is, rather, the condition through which the impossibility of sex becomes installed by the certainty of a love which endures.

In other words, while being a non-haver in love seems to imply a position outside of the comforts of the ego, it could also imply an all the more deceptive forfeiture of love: it is to give the nothing itself as an object, which, in other words, renders *not-having* into another possession or object. In this modality, love, when issued as a demand to an Other, consists of the demand for the nothing as object. This is perhaps among the cleverest ways to cloak castration: by affirming it openly. There is hence an obscene hidden violence inflicted by the lover who wishes for his loved one to give him the love he so demands but also to do so as a free choice. Thus, the loved one is expected to love without any apparent demand to have even done so from the lover. Those who are disinterested in matters concerning love may very well be passionately attached to its demands. The irony is that those who seem most disinterested in love may very well be those who love with the most intensity, those who demand love even more than others. We can imagine the following scenario: a 'bad' guy refuses to pay for lunch, refuses to give flowers or compliments, or to give his attention, and simply waits for his lover to give him the love in spite of it all. In this way, the 'bad' guy can be sure of the authenticity of his lover's gestures. Love is always best tested through the establishment of a zone of nothingness.

This is one of the many reasons that the work of Jacques-Alain Miller is so important today. Miller returns to the early Lacanian topic of love and its relationship with 'the nothing' as object. He writes:

> That underscores love as a paradoxical demand for the gift of nothing. This obviously presupposes that we give this nothing a certain consistency. This is really what Lacan did by calling it 'the nothing' and by making this nothing precisely the object that responds to the demand for this or that [...] the nothing is the object functioning in the

demand for love. [...] in love the Other gives its own lack, that is, its castration. (Jacques-Alain Miller, 2018: 36-8)

To be a 'non-haver' in love can therefore also mean that one is situated within the domain of ego-love by way of the logic of consistency. When we affix the definite article to 'nothing' – *the* nothing – we render it into an imaginary object: the nothing is an object which stands in for the real thing, as a shield against any encounter with the traumatic void. Hence, even in our effort to overcome the logic of possession and consistency in love we seem to reintroduce it through the back door. Not only do we reintroduce it, but we do so in an even more deceptive way. This explains why Lacan claimed that the anorexic eats 'the nothing': the nothing is a shield against a much more traumatic and encounter with jouissance which would completely erase the subject. The nothing as object is exemplified through the apparent rejection of food, it offers protection from the asphyxiated Otherness of the food-objects which would erase the subject's lack-in-being. The paradox is that the subject feels too connected to the food objects. The anorexic simply eats the nothing as a defence against the trauma of there being a lack of lack. The nothing is the anorexic's symptomatic solution to the problem of the intensity of his or her primary social bond: by rejecting food he or she opens up a space for subjectivity as such, for desire, and, indeed, for a love without asphyxiation.

In his fourth seminar, Lacan stated that:

[T]here is in fact in the gift of love only something given 'for nothing,' and which can only be 'nothing.' In other words, it is only provided that a subject gives something freely, that he gives all that he lacks, that the primitive gift [...] is established [so that he] makes the sacrifice beyond what he has. [...] I beg you to consider that if we suppose that a subject has apprehended all possible possessions, all riches, all of that which can be the height of what one may have, then a gift coming from such a subject would literally have no value as a sign of love.

In this statement there is a sign of Lacan's relationship to Georges Bataille. Bataille famously developed a theory of the social bond based upon mutual sacrifice, or 'potlatch.' This new economic perspective, under the name of the 'general economy,' was believed by Bataille to provide the foundation for all of economic exchange. Thus, any 'exchange theory' account of love can be subverted by beginning with the assumption of the sharing of lack. This supposition is an important one for the following reason: we discover that a man who gives all of what he has in love therefore leaves no room for the woman to desire him. This is why the second part of Lacan's statement is important: 'love is giving what one doesn't have ... to somebody who doesn't want it.' This is the mark of man's crucial failure in love: perhaps to be a 'non-haver' in love does not mean that we should give 'the nothing,' but rather it might imply that even when we think we are giving nothing in love we are perhaps all the more giving something. As Jerry Seinfeld once put it: 'nothing is still something!'

3. Love's Twin Axioms

These twin axioms – love as 'non-having' and love as compensation for 'lack' – are not meant to be read as normative statements. Perhaps the point is that we cannot help but be determined by them. To be a 'non-haver' in love is an attempt to provide the space within which love might triumphantly unfold. But the problem is that we have only renewed the fundamental problem and reactivated the determinations of the ego in purer form. It is by positivizing nothing that we can use a false sense of lack as a weapon against lack, and so we do not, in the final instance, master lack. Lack resists mastery, absolutely. Bruce Fink remarks upon the ego defences of pious monks: '[o]ne might have to watch out for a tendency to present oneself as a master at non-mastery, like that found in certain spiritual practices, and akin to the tendency to promote oneself as the most humble of the humble in certain religious groups' (Fink, 2014: xiii-xiv). This was also the strategy pursued by many on the anarchist revolutionary left. The question becomes: how can we defend against the temptation to move too hastily against love as possession into a strategy of love as consistency (e.g., the nothing object)? Similarly, how can we keep ourselves from simply repeating, pathologically, love as possession?

The movement from possession to consistency was the strategy I used for at least a decade of anarchist organizing. Within the anarchist subculture one of the best ways to obtain authority, or, rather, to become respected and to have one's voice and discourse appreciated is to make a pretense at 'non-mastery.' Anarchist politics often consists of demonstrating more than any Other that one is not at all a master, that one is not at all contaminated by statist or bourgeois desires – that one has, to borrow a wonderful expression from the post-anarchist theory (and friend) Saul Newman, a 'pure and uncontaminated point of departure for politics outside of power' (Newman, 2001). Indeed, some of the post-anarchists (Saul Newman, Todd May, Richard J. F. Day, and others) attempt to demonstrate the paradoxical nature of this pursuit (ibid). It is by embarking upon this pursuit toward an uncontaminated and pure place of non-mastery that the subject renews his authority and influence within the anarchist subculture. Indeed, the anarchist today has discovered that his discourse is perfectly suited to university discourse, such that anarchists are today one of the leading intellectual discourses within Humanities, Liberal Arts, and Social Science departments. Once, during an intense session with my first psychoanalyst, I blurted out the following: 'I could be the master by pretending not to be!' The statement seemed to have come from another place, since I was not expecting to say it. I realized that it was a foundational axiom which governed my life for decades of political organizing. It involved, much like my eating disorder, the positivization of *non-being*: 'I could be ... by *not-being*.' This helps us to understand what Hegel and Slavoj Žižek mean when they claim that a true master gives absolute freedom.

Bruce Fink was describing a tendency to positive the real of *objet petit a* as semblance and to approach love as a non-dupe. Yet, for this type of love one cannot be a non-dupe: anarchists are

51

so keen on outrunning the discourse of mastery that they imagine themselves outside of it and thereby renew their fundamental deception. This is why Lacan claimed that, 'revolutionary aspirations have only one possibility: always to end up in the discourse of the master. Experience has proven this. What you aspire to as revolutionaries is a master. You will have one!' (as cited in Stavrakakis, 1999: 12). It is the same in love: those who believe themselves to be 'non-dupes' of love and the discourse of mastery in fact 'err,' since, as Lacan proclaimed, it is the 'non-dupes who err.' However, is it not the case that today one *must* become a non-dupe in love in order to counteract the wider society which requests them no longer to be duped by love? To be a non-dupe in love today is to affirm a certainty in love against the temptation to never fall in love at all. This is the new modality of love emerging today: to refuse to be a dupe in love as a clinical technique. Those trapped within the whirlwind of temptation may find a mode of stabilization in their non-dupery, and therefore, also, the possibility of subjective rectification. Put another way, it is by voluntarily duping oneself in love that one can introduce a zone of desire essential for the perpetuation of the love encounter.

Love has always been distinguished from 'lust' and 'temptation' within religious, philosophical, and classical texts. There is also always a warning of the dangers of lust and temptation, even when 'lust' is not presumed to be literally sexual in nature. Within the Bible, the English translation of 'lust,' from Hebrew, does not capture what is actually going on: lust in the Bible not at all associated with sexual desire – though it may nonetheless be related to the Freudian or Lacanian notion of 'sex' – but rather to heightened and unrestrained attraction, especially to beauty: for example, there is, in Proverbs 6:25, 'lust not after her beauty in thine heart; neither (let her) take thee with (her) eyelids.' This 'eyes so that they *may not see*' position releases us from the temptation to restrict beauty and lust to love yet it also leaves us fundamentally unanchored. Is lust not another name for the Lacanian notion of drive? Yet, at the same time, it also seems connected to a notion of the sensible and intelligible. Moreover, the drives – lusts, if you like and their sometimes associated erotomania – are central to the experience of that unanchored mental structure known as psychosis (Vanheule, 2011). How shall we proceed on the question of the relationship of lust to love?

Lust could be associated with psychotic loss, the loss of any central symbolic prohibition. There is within the various stanzas of Dante's *Inferno,* dedicated to the experience of falling into the second circle of hell, a striking example of these new temptations. They seem to take on the structure Lacan's controversial and underdeveloped fifth discourse, named 'capitalist discourse.' The fifth discourse is perhaps exemplary of a principle of lust and should be related to the Freudian *lustprinzip* ('pleasure-principle') since it also is an instinctive defence against the jouissance of the drive. The *lustprinzip* operates within capitalist discourse as if it had not yet encountered the adequacy of any *realitatsprinzip* ('reality-principle'); indeed, the *realitatsprinzip* seems to concern precisely the structure of a certain gap or distance within which the subject might emerge. Under capitalist discourse these two principles seem no longer to function in a final determinant and consistent manner, but rather through a constant reactivation and rediscovery of reality. The endless cycle of losing reality within capitalism results not in subjectivity destitution but rather in the destitution of subjectivity itself. In other words, the problem is that the subject is produced only as a fleeting experience. Thus, to borrow an expression from Alain Badiou: there are many objects in a world but the difficulty is to see how a subject can emerge from all of this.

The *Inferno* laments the triumph of the sexual over the parallax distance that any 'fall' in love might have offered. It is a poem about the loss of love's fall rather than the loss of the subject's choice to fall in love. Therefore, once again, we witness in the *Inferno* a fundamentally ontological statement regarding love, rather than a normative one: the loss of love is the loss of the ability to lose itself, and this gives rise to a whirlwind of temptations which operate according to the intensity of the drives within the real. Dante wrote that there is an 'infernal hurricane, which never rests, drives the spirits onward in violence; whirling them around [and around], it molests [tortures] them' (Dante, 1995: 5: 31-33).

This 'infernal hurricane which never rests' is none other than the movement of the capitalist discourse which, as Lacan has put it, 'runs as if it were on wheels, it […] actually runs too fast, it runs out, it runs out such that it burns itself out' (Lacan, 1972: 48). The second layer of hell is perhaps the fastest one: it is a form of suffering from speed, from intensity, from a cycle of the drives which boomerang without producing the requisite subjectivity.

Lacan's fifth discourse, the 'capitalist discourse,' is structured in such a way that the subject moves quickly to avoid subjective destitution. (Often, the subject moves pragmatically, since capitalist discourse seems to have emerged from the influence of the early American pragmatists; see Rousselle, 2019. Yet, one witnesses the same pragmatism, in a more intense form, within Indian cultures, grounded perhaps in the creative-destruction of the Upanishads. It seems to me that postmodern capitalism, liquid modernity, and so on, were already formed within India well before America pushed its way toward it in the 1970's-1990's.) It is perhaps a movement to avoid; since to avoid, in this sense, means that it is a movement to negate the void (e.g., 'a-void'), to outrun the void of subjectivity. Within the sphere of love, capitalist drive is demonstrated in the quick movement from partner to partner, in fleeting romantic encounters, but it is also related to the movement from product to product within the grocery store, from gadget to gadget, upgrade to upgrade, and so on. Pedagogically, capitalist discourse demonstrates itself also in the movement from slide to slide or module to module within the classroom.

Incidentally, university discourse has today mutated within the West. Knowledge – epistemology – does not attain the consistency that it had under tradition universal discourse, before the emergence of neoliberalism or so-called postmodern society as the cultural logic of late capitalism. The student of capitalist discourse prefers to regulate himself according to fleeting aphorisms, witticisms, and words of wisdom. The student today demands chunks of knowledge rather than dogmatic statements that endure throughout the entirety of a course. The professor, succumbing to these demands and also being a product of capitalist discourse, produces modules which act as capsules to quickly medicate the student's thirst for knowledge (see Rousselle, 2019). In India this process was accelerated: whereas the neoliberal university nonetheless retains its textual bureaucratic structure – whereby the content is capitalist – the typical Indian university, from what I can gather through my own experience working within them – has already revolutionized its form: form itself is part of the process of capitalist discourse.

The goal is the subject who loves via capitalist discourse is not to overcome the paternal universal prohibition installed by the name-of-the-father, since he has none. Rather, it is to avoid – to move in haste from the void – through fleeting encounters, wisdoms, and to endlessly 'renew' the relationship. This explains why today's most moving statements are not troubling 'universal prohibitions' in the form of 'you shall not' but rather 'particular affirmative' statements in the form of 'sometimes in life it is okay to ...' This is the discourse exemplified by the popular American television show *Grey's Anatomy*. The medical drama (e.g., props, narrative, setting, roles, etc.) serve to conceal the trauma of subjective destitution. Each episode reaches a fever pitch at the precise moment that the subject encounters her own destitution, and that at that moment when the medical pretence can no longer contain the raw 'real' of the underlying drama/ trauma. This moment is most often indicated by an intensification in background music until it comes to an abrupt and dramatic silence: suddenly a calm reassuring maternal voice speaks from somewhere outside of the frame to provide an essential life lesson.

We should pay close attention to these life lessons because they reveal something essential about life in America. Each lesson functions as a little piece of wisdom meant to retroactively offer a provisional remedy, a 'quick fix,' for subjective destitution. We are treated to such life lessons as 'sometimes the expected simply pales in comparison to the unexpected,' 'sometimes it is good to be scared, it means you still have something to lose,' 'sometimes the future changes quickly and completely and we're left with only the choice of what to do next,' and so on. *Grey's Anatomy* demonstrates how capitalist discourse functions today within the West and how the maternal phallus can become embodied by woman: the paternal signifier would have instigated a universal prohibition against enjoyment (thereby instigating a desire to return to the supposed enjoyment that has been lost) but instead we see the rise of the particular affirmative injunction to enjoy. 'You shall not ...' has become replaced by 'sometimes you should ..' and 'maybe it is okay that ...' These imaginary fixes are as temporary; when the old wisdom has become worn out there is already a new one (which may contradict the previous) prepared in advance for our direct consumption.

But what about capitalist discourse in India? It is clear to me that it does not function with the moment of symbolic re-anchoring, but rather it keeps moving, faster than we thought hitherto possible. Unlike *Grey's Anatomy*, Bollywood movies seem to demonstrate that symbolic narrative matters very little with respect to the real of the musical emotional intensity and the phantasy of *never giving up* in spite of the impossibility of this or that circumstance. The confluence of music and image demonstrates that even image is subservient to and guided by an underlying real affective intensity. Thus, the cinematic genius of Bollywood is to place music at the center and to have the film – its moving images, and its narrative content – strictly subservient and consequential to the intensity of the invocatory drive. Indeed, I witnessed on several occasions during my visit to Indian theatres the intense connection of Indian audiences to the musical content of the film: there is an insistence upon ignoring the symbolic narrative (e.g., people are talking throughout the entire film, or looking away, or on their phones, etc.) and yet arising and dancing or singing along with the musical content. Indian cultures thus 'play it by ear' while the American Hollywood cultures are closer to a preference for the image.

In any case, Dante continued: 'lovers [are] adrift into self-indulgence and were carried away by their passions, so now they drift forever. The bright, voluptuous sin is now seen as it is: a howling darkness of helpless discomfort.' The subject of love remains within the whirlwind of temptation, ever suspicious of love because it appears to him for what it is: a howling darkness of helpless discomfort. He rejects love's inherent fall, and therefore spirals endlessly until he finally burns himself out and witnesses the truth: this cycle of lust and temptation were inadequate attempts to avoid the traumatic void itself, a void which can never be outrun, no matter how fast one moves. The foreclosure of love is therefore also the possible birth of a certainty against the certain rejection of the pain of love's fall. Today we often prefer to put our careers and personal happiness before love: we require a partner who will supplement our already existing temptations (e.g., career aspirations, friendship networks, family life, and so on). We increasingly see love as a distraction or obstacle to these things and so foreclosure that obstacle. Is it any wonder that American newly-weds increasingly opt to get married alone – they marry themselves, or else they marry without family present, and so on – or they choose to go on honeymoons independent of their spouses?

One might expect this trend to gain popularity within the coming decades in America. The 'solo-moon' is an emerging American practice whereby newly-weds respect the mutual wishes of each partner's desire for personal happiness and self-love. It offers a break from the sweetness of the honeymoon. At one time the honeymoon offered people the sweetness of pleasure, yet today Americans are moving toward more Middle Eastern (primarily Islamic) practices whereby during and immediately after the marriage the sexes split from one another. At the beginning of my previous marriage, an Islamic marriage (which was the result of an ultimatum by her parents: 'marry her or else lose her forever'), I recall an entire evening alone in my tuxedo in a strange café in Tripoli, Lebanon. My then-wife celebrated alone with her family and friends. These social bonds intend to manage the 'too-muchness' of the sexual relationship after the loss of love's fall. Today's capitalist 'hook-up' culture necessitates a practice of distance, revealing that the only option left on the table today is to fall in love again, but this time as a certainty. Arthur Rimbaud's misinterpreted words should today be misinterpreted even better: He says: 'I don't love women. Love has to be reinvented, we know that.' Love as certainty – the affirmative love of woman as a symptom – can help us defend and endure against the whirlwind of the maternal capitalist demand that we enjoy our various temptations.

4. Forfeiting Love

There is an interesting connection of eating disorders such as anorexia to traumas in love. I have suffered for as long as I can remember from anorexia. Since the time of Freud, there has been a concern that eating disorders are related to psychotic states. One of the 'primal scenes' for an eating disorder might be as follows: two brothers who are in rivalry with each other for the attention of their mother recognize that food can be used to solicit her love. One brother receives the mother's love through acceptance of her demand to eat, but the other finds that it is by rejecting food that he can obtain even more love than his brother. By not eating, which does not imply a rejection of food but rather a positivization of lack via the food's object-relation, one can receive a more genuine form of love: 'Oh, dear son, I care so much for you, so would you please eat for me?' The subject now feels love from the mother which was absent, and he is rewarded for his positivization of lack precisely by way of more attention. The anorexic is not the one who has *rejected* food as a bond based on love (as is commonly claimed). Rather, the anorexic is the one who realizes more than any other subject that food is a bond based upon love: he renews his demand for love by eating 'the nothing' itself.

Lacan's famous claim is as follows:

> [For] anorexia nervosa [...] the resistance to omnipotence in the relationship of dependence develops under the sign of [the] nothing into a cancellation of the object as symbolic; it is at the level of the object that the child puts in check his dependence, and precisely by feeding on anything, he even reverses his relation of dependence by making the master eager to make *him* live – from which he depends on her desire.

The anorexic transforms the symbolic object – the master signifier, or the 'no' of the father (the signifier of universal prohibition over the mother's desire) – into a semblance by rendering it into a self-made consistency of nothingness. Nothing becomes *the nothing* as proper name and it structures the relationship of the subject to his desire via the detour of love. The nothing becomes an invention fashioned so as to metaphorize – that is, substitute and distance – the proximity of the Other. Typically, the 'no' or 'name' of the father functions to separate and therefore substitute the proximity of the mother's desire for language and speech. However, when this fails, it is possible to compensate through the logic of artistic invention. Thus, Jacques-Alain Miller claims, in light of Lacan's statement that 'one can make-do without the Name-of-the-Father provided it is put to use' (Lacan, 2016), that:

> [There can be] a substituted substitute. The name-of-the-father substitutes itself for the desire of the mother, imposes its order on the desire of the mother, and what we call the predicate of the name-of-the-father is an element which is a kind of make-believe of the name-of-the-father, a *compensatory make-believe* of the name-of-the-father – the *CMB*. [...] [We could] make a complete list of all the possible forms of Compensatory Make-Believes in psychosis!' (Miller, 2015: 153)

We have within the field of the eating disorders the compensatory mechanism of the self-made 'no' to food objects. In this case, it is not therefore that food objects provide some temporary comfort for the subject who so desires to return to the primordial mother. Rather, the subject finds comfort precisely in the inadequacy of the mother's connection – the subject seeks to emerge through the traumatic window of nothingness itself. It is in the darkness that the subject emerges finally as an emptiness. In one case, it becomes affirmed in the anorexic subject's given name: 'Duane,' which means, 'Dark' or 'Darkness.' The nothing achieves the dignity of a proper name or noun and structures a relationship with the Other through the detour of love.

This process instills a paradoxical desire, which, in of itself, is the installation also of a new domain of suffering. There are lovers who suffer in order to avoid an altogether more traumatic suffering. The suffering is bad, but it could be worse. Indeed, this is what we learn from Lacan's seminar ... *Or Worse*. We might claim that today's lovers suffer more than any other, they have it for the worst: they are offered the ability to suffer precisely as a defence against trauma – they suffer not from doubts in love but rather by the certainty of their love. Freud did not go far enough when he hypothesized that eating disorders are 'reactions of protest against anxiety,' and when he wrote the following:

> The function of nutrition is most frequently disturbed by a disinclination to eat, brought about by a withdrawal of libido. An increase in the desire to eat is also a not uncommon thing. The compulsion to eat is attributed to a fear of starving [lack]; but this is a subject which has been but little studied. The hysterical defence against eating is known to us in the symptom of vomiting. Refusal to eat owing to anxiety is a concomitant of psychotic states (delusions of being poisoned). (Freud, 1949)

Most interesting is that Freud eventually linked these statements to ego symptoms. Just a few sentences later he wrote: 'our survey might be extended to other functions of the ego as well' (ibid). The Freudian theory of inhibitions – as that which exists within the various clinical structures of neurosis, both hysterical and obsessional, and psychosis – harkens us to situate the nothing object differently with respect to the various modalities of love. Psychotic nothingness is certainly different from the nothing object at play in the various neuroses.

The altogether more troubling possibility exists today that one has already forfeited the very desire to *have* a partner in love. In other words, there has been a forfeiture of forfeiture itself, a relinquishment of the possibility of relinquishing. Put another way, it is a fall from the fall or a 'lack of lack.' This possibility is related fundamentally to the sort of whirlwind of jouissance associated with addictions and other enjoyable forms of suffering. The Canadian comedian Norm Macdonald outlined this paradoxical dimension of 'jouissance' operating within addictions:

> [My friend] has the disease of alcoholism. And he came to me, and he told me. I'm the kind of guy who likes to look on the bright

side of things. So I told him, I said: 'Richie, it's true that you have a disease and everything, but I think you have the best one!'

The addicted subject is a happy subject in the sense that he exists like Joker: suffering from the enjoyment which compels him, suffering from his smiles and laughter. The upsurge of jouissance associated with the 'lack of lack' is also related to the void or hole which persists and drives the subject desperately toward his various temptations. Until he burns out, or until he finds his castrating certainty.

These twin threats therefore exist: first, there is the temptation to exchange an authentic encounter (love's fall) for various divergent temptations, and/or; second, there is the loss of the various loss of love, the loss of the foundation upon which any failure in love depends. Alfred Lord Tennyson's famous aphorism – 'This better to have loved and lost, then never to have loved at all' – therefore requires updating. First, we need to think deeply about what it means to 'have' love, since, immediately, this seems more and more contradictory. Second, we cannot claim that love exists without losing since losing is essential to the experience of love. And, third, it seems to me that the final clause should rather be written as '…than never to have had the possibility of losing loss itself.' In one failure, there is the temptation to disallow the fall of the ego into the id, and, in the other failure, there is a concern of the inadequacy of the ego of love itself (e.g., its endurance in time, its consistency, its body, etc.

Thus, if in Christianity the body of Christ has been lost and resurrected (and then lost again), then, in Islam there is often the claim that the body of Christ will return again. Why do most Muslims believe that the body of Jesus will return? My claim is that it is because Islam reveals another dimension of Christianity, a Christianity which is more Christian than Christianity itself: Christianity describes the process through which the body of Christ might be resurrected, but Islam describes the inevitable return of a body from the real of capitalist discourse itself. Abu Huraira has said of Islam's final prophet: 'Allah's Apostle said, 'the hour will not be established until the son of Mary (i.e. Jesus) descends amongst you as a just ruler, he will break the cross, kill the pigs, and abolish the Jizya tax. Money will be in abundance so that nobody will accept it.' Islamic eschatology sometimes claims that Jesus will emerge from within the 'arcades' (shopping mall) to finally reveal the truth of Quranic doctrine – he will therefore be a Muslim Jesus, an anti-capitalist Jesus, a communist Jesus. And he will be a Jesus whose body will unite the Ummah in a final worldwide *ummah* (community/body of believers). This position seems to me to be perfectly consistent with Marx's claim that communism emerges from within Capitalist political economy. Put another way, communism shall emerge from within the shopping malls.

These twin tendencies in love persist. The psychoanalytic clinic seems to demonstrate that the latter type of love – the love of certainty – is becoming more and more the dominant condition. Though there is a receding familial and social structure anchored to the first threat, the contemporary structure ensures that today's subjects love with certainty and conviction or else they do not love at all. Thus, the hegemonic position today is to not fall in love at all. My fundamental conviction is that love in the contemporary period shall survive as a certainty and that it may become the only means through which humans can produce a social bond that is lacking. The certainty of love might erect a fundamental failure for which the subject will bemoan but will not do without. More and more, we require subjects to suffer from their certainties and love seems to me to be the principal site through which this certainty might be meaningfully explored and expressed. The demand to be loved has increasingly become replaced by the threat that love not arise at all; such that, with luck, it arises only as a pure certainty, only as an unshakable conviction. Moreover, it arises as a certainty for which the subject emerges as such, as a suffering subject, who retroactively posits the very causality of his passions.

III

Communication

1. What Does Sociology Communicate About Love?

What (and how) does sociology communicate about love? Broadly speaking, classical sociologists came from one of the following three major schools of thought: first, there were those who believed that society consists of nothing more than the multiplicity of interactions among its constituent parts; second, there were those who proposed that society is a transcendental whole greater than the sum of its parts and a reality sui generis, and; third, there were those who argued that society is repeatedly – I would add also that it is tenuously and fleetingly – reproduced as a consequence of pragmatic truth-oriented activity. The first approach was put forward by such German sociologists as Max Weber and Georg Simmel, and later formed under the banner of 'symbolic interactionism' by Herbert Blumer. Before Blumer transformed German sociology into a distinctively American pragmatic endeavour, there was the belief in an immanent chaos of the social world. This noumenal chaos could be understood in some sense through empathetic understanding via the construction of 'ideal-types' (for Max Weber) and the 'social forms' of interaction (for Georg Simmel). We should locate the true reference points for the third approach in the work of George Herbert Mead and Charles Horton Cooley. This is the approach of early American pragmatists out of Chicago and Michigan. Finally, the second approach, that of positivism, was championed by such French thinkers as Auguste Comte and Emile Durkheim, both of whom aimed to empirically study 'social facts.'

These three schools of classical sociology defined the terrain and set the tone for what came after within the various academic disciplines of sociology. It is often expected that contemporary students of sociology anchor themselves to one of these three schools before pursuing their own unique and subtle variations. It is striking that each of these approaches nonetheless resembles a wider discourse from which it emerged. It is as if each school focused on exploring and widening the scope of a pre-existing postulate or code inherited from their own social environment. The Germans valued introspection and speculation, the French accelerated 'secularist' values (exemplified in 'laicite'), and American attitudes were related to a Calvinist capitalist spirit or ethos (see Rousselle, 2019). This mirrors to some extent the ideal-type famously outlined by Slavoj Žižek:

> In a traditional German toilet, the hole, into which shit disappears after we flush, is right at the front, so that shit is first laid out for us to sniff and inspect for traces of illness. In the typical French toilet, on the contrary, the hole is at the back (i.e., shit is supposed to disappear as quickly as possible). Finally, the American (Anglo-Saxon) toilet presents a synthesis, a mediation between these opposites: the toilet basin is full of water, so that the shit floats in it, visible, but not to be inspected. […] Hegel was among the first to see in the geographical triad of Germany, France, and England, an expression of three different existential attitudes: reflective thoroughness (German), revolutionary hastiness (French), and utilitarian pragmatism (English). In political terms, this triad can be read as German conservatism, French revolutionary radicalism, and English liberalism. […] [we can] identify its underlying mechanism in the three different attitudes towards excremental excess: an ambiguous contemplative fascination; a wish to get rid of it as fast as possible; a pragmatic decision to treat it as ordinary and dispose of it in an appropriate way (Žižek, unpublished).

Žižek was here adopting a resolutely German attitude, following, as it were, the methodological assumptions of the sociologist Max Weber in constructing an ideal-type. However, Žižek does so with a certain revolutionary energy that we might find among the French: Ideal-typical toilets reveal an underlying ideological symbolic structure which in some way defines a culture according to the discourse of its social bond. Thus, each position only renewed the environmental codes or ideological doctrines which were unknowingly internalized. Or, to put it another way, each school of sociology remains within the sphere of an overarching communicative context such that it seems representative of precisely that which it claims to be exploring and analyzing. A discourse cannot get outside of itself to witness its situatedness within the environment which it tasks itself to explain.

Currently, the only counter-point to the determinations of the environment or to discourse discovered has been psychoanalytic discourse (Lacan, 2007: 99). It alone has found a mode of discourse which does not renew the prevailing environmental conditions, codes, or configurations which determine it. By configuration, I mean to state that discourse is a mode of subjective insertion within the social bond. For Lacan, discourse is itself a social bond, founded upon language (Lacan, 1991 [1969]). However, I am not satisfied with this word 'founded' because it implies that language precedes the social bond, when, in fact, language is often the basis or outcome of the establishment of a social bond. This is a point made very well recently by Slavoj Žižek: it is not that language has no beginning but rather that once it has established itself – once the symbolic order has set in – in retroactively produces its own timelessness (Žižek, 2019). This sort of transcendental illusion conceals its own immanent fragility. In any case, discourse outlines a number of communicative configurations of codes or signifiers vis-à-vis an environment or Other, and it is this relationship to the environment or Other which demonstrates its social significance.

Traditionally, we would claim that it is only the psychotic who is without discourse because for her there is no isolatable and external environment or Other. The psychotic is either completely disconnected from the Other or else feels herself completely taken by the Other. There is no Other because there is only Other. We can locate a modest sociological proof – but one that I think is nonetheless interesting and inventive – for this claim in Emile Durkheim's famous chart on suicide. Durkheim aimed to study the following social facts in relation to one another: social integration, social regulation, suicide, and religion. As most students of classical or modern sociology are aware, there are two axes: on the 'y' axis, there is more or less 'social regulation,' and on the 'x' axis there is more or less 'social integration.' These twin 'social facts' govern and determine the type and prevalence of suicide within an environment, or, put another way, they are in fact the determinations of the environment upon the subject who may or may not be prone to suicidal ideation.

When the subject is too integrated to the environment there is a type of suffering that Durkheim refers to as altruistic. This is a type of trauma that occurs due to the loss of self to the overarching group. The self dissolves into the group. On the other hand, when the child is separated from social objects in the environment, a selfish ego forms and inspires his return to the perceived lost environmental connection. This, of course, is the classical Freudian narrative: the subject, unable to maturely cope with castration anxiety – his cut from the social bond – desires a return to an oceanic feeling of harmony and union. On the axis of integration, then, there is an implicit maternal connection to jouissance. This connection is capable of engulfing and destroying the subject's individuality. The consequent trauma produces all sorts of new problems in the social bond – what today clinicians refer to as the 'new symptoms' – because it forecloses the fact of social regulation. On the other hand, classical symptoms occur when the subject has already exchanged this maternal jouissance for the regulation of the signifier. A different relationship to suffering is thereby constructed: what Durkheim named 'egoistic suicide' occurs not from the trauma of jouissance but rather from the suffering of isolation, from the longing to re-establish a social bond one believes that one has lost, or, in other words, from the fact of desire.

However, there can also be a 'double rejection' of trauma, a situation described by Slavoj Žižek as 'redoubled lack' or by

Jacques Lacan as 'lack of lack.' Whereas the trauma of jouissance occurs when the subject rejects the suffering of desire – the rejection of desire comes first as a foreclosure of social grammar, that is, of the laws of social interaction; in other words, as the foreclosure of social regulation – the subject can also opt, after this foreclosure and consequent 'redoubled lack,' to reject trauma itself. Durkheim's analysis therefore requires a third axis, the 'z' axis, which is related to the Lacanian 'imaginary.' The axis of integration seems to imply something relating to the real whereby 'too much integration' is a real proximity of the 'maternal thing' (which implies the loss of subjectivity), and 'not enough integration' is a real of desire as objet petit a (social regulation produces a feeling of not enough integration and a desire to return to the oceanic feeling of proximity). The axis of regulation relates to the relative rise and fall of the paternal signifier, the name/no-of-the-father. The subject who has rejected the paternal signifier and cleaves to maternal jouissance finds himself at the bottom left quadrant of the suicide chart, without subjectivity and without an environment or social bond. Yet, the subject might avoid the trauma and push forward on the 'z' axis. This movement occurs by way of 'making-do without the paternal signifier, yet producing, nonetheless, one's own paternal signifier through the imaginary: it is the discovery of the beauty of codes and sign languages.

Discourse – whose ingredients are either signifiers or signs/codes – are important for understanding society but they are also important for situating sociological theory itself. A key aspect of Lacanian discourse analysis is that in every case the social bond of discourse is also a mode of symptomatic stabilization for the subject vis-à-vis the real significations of his environment. Every discourse is a triumph against the confluence of symbolic and real through unique cultural configurations which find a way to live with the unlivable; yet, only analytic discourse begins up front with the fact of the domain of the real. For example, the discourse of the master produces the real as a consequence of the slave's submission to an imaginary pact (e.g., 'a peace treaty'). The slave desires to be set free, to return to the conditions of what Bracha L. Ettinger refers to as its 'matrixial environment,' and yet does not realize that this semblance of freedom nonetheless is the integrity for the perpetuation of his slavery. The university discourse engages directly with the real in its manifold presentations: as that which resists symbolization, absolutely, and yet, also as that which gives rise to imaginary consistencies and predictability by way of ego knowledge. Finally, the discourse of the hysteric demands from the master an account of his ethical responsibility without recognizing that the real desire implicit in this demand conceals an inescapable deadlock. Thus, the real persists, despite desire, through desire, as the push of a limit and hole within, before, and beyond any social stabilization.

Sociological theory is always situated within an overarching discourse which sustains it. American sociology has produced one of the most innovative solutions to the problem of the real by blending the university and the hysteric discourses into a new mutation: 'capitalist discourse,' Lacan's fifth discourse (see Rousselle, 2019). Capitalist discourse accommodates the real through the endless circulation of lathouses. These are ready-made objects which may be picked-up and abandoned on whim as the subject moves endlessly through the market-place of his academic life. Inevitably, the subject burns out on capitalist. Burnout or depression are inevitable by-products of a discourse which moves too fast. Once again, the only counter-point too all of this has been the analyst's discourse which begins already with the presupposition that the social bond of discourse is based upon a primordial trauma, loss, or limit which can never be surpassed except by admitting up front that it is the foundation.

This lesson is important for classical and contemporary sociological theory. Take as a case the popular work on love by the German sociological theorist Niklas Luhmann. If Emile Durkheim attempted to demonstrate the singularity of sociological discourse in his book Suicide (1897) (by showing how an apparently personal and emotional state can be studied sociologically and hence independently of the psyches of those who commit to suicide), then Luhmann attempted to make a similar intervention with the topic of love in his book Love as Passion: The Codification of Intimacy (1982). Durkheim's study proved the worthiness of the academic discipline of sociology through his non-biological, non-psychology, and non-philosophical study of suicide as a 'social fact.' Similarly, Luhmann showed that love should not be confined to a mere philosophical or psychological exploration of love's affective capacity, but rather as a social bond grounded upon symbolic communication:

> [L]ove will not be treated here as a feeling (or at least only secondarily so), but rather in terms of its constituting a symbolic code which shows how to communicate effectively in situations where this would otherwise appear improbable. The code thus encourages one to have the appropriate feelings. (1998: 8-9)

For Luhmann, the affective life associated with love is determined by a volatile code, such that, love is based upon a discourse which constitutes its social bond.

2. What is a Code?

In his Luhmann Lexicon (2005), Krause explains that a code has 'a binary foundational difference or a bi-stable form for generating binary distinctions. Codes are always bivalent, [they] have a positive and negative value' (Krause, 2005: 132). We should begin by recognizing that despite all of the fashionable rejections of binaries within academia, there is nonetheless something important about rejecting the rejection of a binary. After all, scission, the finding of a 'two' is what produces the 'one' which those deconstructionists so naively presuppose to be at the foundation of the cut of two. All of logic today seems to demonstrate that we must first be capable of counting to two before we can accept any semblance of one. Put psychoanalytically, one is the fantasy of a primordial harmony produces from the fact of there being two. A code, which is another form of 'two,' is therefore responsible for igniting and setting into motion an entire communicative apparatus based upon its primordial foundational difference, or what Francois Laurelle might have called its 'decisional structure' (Laruelle, 2013). The political communicative sphere consists of a foundational code which renders everything into 'powerful' or else 'powerless,' scientific communication consists of an engagement with 'truths' and 'non-truths,' and so on. It therefore appears as though Luhmann has opened up a 'symbolic unconscious' within a communicative system. Thus, each system of communication 'interprets' its environment according to these binary foundational differences, and the only way to become aware of these determinations is to identify them, as Luhmann does, as the fundamental phantasy governing an entire system.

I do not believe this is the entire story on codes and binary distinctions. First of all, the logic of a code is different from the logic of a signifier. The 'master signifier' of the name/no-of-the-father is responsible for prohibiting connections to the maternal environment. The subject of the system thereby achieves relative autonomy from his matrixial/maternal environment because of the non-sensical name/no-of-the-father. There are nonetheless cases where this symbolic function of the name/no-of-the-father fails at some level, when, for example, the master signifier offers an affirmation as well as a prohibition. In such cases, the bivalence of the code ensures that the subject remains radically ambivalence – or, 'bivalent' – with respect to the paternal signifier. It is when there is radical ambivalence that we can refer to a 'code' rather than a 'master signifier,' since codes do not provide universal prohibitions for the subject but rather offers a volatile connection to the chaotic matrixial environment. Thus, I distinguish between the logic of a 'code' and the logic of a 'signifier,' since the former remains problematically 'one' and hence does not have the retroactive determinations of cut from 'two;' put another way, a code is a 'one' which is incapable of knowing that it is one all alone.

The subject of the code cannot help but encounter a dizzying array of ostensibly non-localizable signifiers/codes within his environment. Is this not also the example that has been observed in the various modalities of the clinical structure known as psychosis? Codes are holophrastic and indicative of object-ambivalence. Whereas the paternal signifier should have cancelled the mother's desire by exchanging it for a body of signifiers, the code retains a connection to the matrixial/maternal environment (whereby this environment is also the mother's desire). A code speaks only to itself by interacting with and instigating the noise of its environment while also rejecting and foreclosing it. On the other hand, a signifier separates the subject from the matrixial environment and instigates an endless desire to return back that which has been lost. If the subject of the signifier asks 'what am I to my environment?' then the subject of a code asks 'how is the environment simply an extension of myself?' A code is therefore always proof of a degree of primordial foreclosure of the environment and yet it is also the mechanism through which the auto-poietic system further propels itself. For Luhmann, then, there is a fragility to the subject – so much so that there is a question of whether subjectivity exists at all within a communicative system. It is well known that Luhmann resists any discussion of subjects or individuals and remains only at the abstract level of communicative competency. As in psychosis, the problem is not of subjective destitution but of the destitution of the subject itself. The problem for the communicative system is to produce within itself a zone of distance within which the subject should inhabit.

Within a Luhmannian system, the subject has vanished from the scene, replaced by a delusional and delirious system of circulating codes which are themselves forever threatened by an environment which the system itself projects out into the real. The environment is nothing but a delusion of a system, a delusion which is at once complicated, confusing, and threatening. At any moment the pressure of the environment might senselessly intrude and castrate the system, devouring it in its entirety. A system's only recourse is to remain in fidelity to its own holophrastic certainties, since delusion is at the center of any communicative system: these certainties find within the noise of the environment the possibility of their own dilation, an expansion of their scope, an inflation of their certainty, an extension of their presupposed meaning. We become witnesses to our own environment without realizing that these external manifestations were built to be tested by the power of our own interpretation. Thus, Stijn Vanheule wrote that 'the subject in psychosis [is] a martyr of the unconscious, a passive witness of strange messages that come from without' (2011: 79). If indeed a subject exists at all then it 'has its cause in its own pocket' (Lacan, 1966-7), each communicative 'sphere' constructs its own symbolic causation, its own environmental determinations.

These internal codes serve as a response to that which pushes its way through as an ostensibly external void. Codes always remain trapped within their internal auto-poietic systems. They resist symbolic signification, absolutely, and yet come to stand in place of them. When the symbolic is foreclosed it returns nonetheless within the real; foreclosure of the paternal signifier ensures that castration will return in the real as a certainty. The noise of the environment is always the ultimate threat to any communicative system. Intersubjectivity is therefore a mode of neurotic desire – there is a desire to return to the maternal environment from which the subject has been separated – and auto-poietic invention is the mode of defence for the psychotic subject. Since the name/no-of-the-father has been foreclosed, the subject projects himself through endless boundary-maintenance (without ever being able to adequately do it). This is also the cause of a system's object ambivalence. Contemporary sociologists have been enthralled by the so-called 'epistemological constructivism' of Luhmann's approach without recognizing that the 'highest system,' namely the 'cultural system,' indicates a defensive self-referentiality forever pitted against the void of the Other. While this has served as a nice alternative to the intersubjective approach of Habermas, it has not solved the problem of the void itself.

Self-referential systems expand in scope only by fashioning innovative interpretations of the signifiers circulating within their environment and by reducing them in some way to an affirmation or negation of central static code. Anthony King wrote:

> [T]he steering of any system is not consequently the result of conscious social interaction, but rather the automatic, self-transforming responses of the system to the communication it receives. In Luhmann's sociology, human social interaction is effaced in favour of a self-equilibrating and self-transforming system. Autopoiesis is not reducible to the social relations between humans; nor does it ultimately

depend upon human consciousness. Luhmann's work promotes a stern form of ontological dualism in which the individual is subordinated to the objective system. (2004: 10)

In this reading, the environment is in fact determinative, and not, as it were, the autonomous or 'conscious' communicative gestures of the system itself. We should go even further here: it is not that the individual and his relations are subordinated to the environment (since this would presume the ontological existence of a subject) but rather that the subject – as a lack within the system – is not at all operative. The subject may only be said to be operative through a separation from environment, and this separation can only occur by way of a prohibition of fusion with that environment. Yet, for Luhmann, it is clear that the Other's prohibition has been foreclosed in advance by any given system. All of Luhmann's systems are therefore psychotic – and this is unlike psychoanalytic thought, where systems exist according to differing discursive structures. There is within all of this a profound paradox: although the subject has been overdetermined by his environment – indeed, he has been effectively erased – there is nonetheless a radical defence on the part of the system against that very environment. How might we account for this paradox? We might begin by marking the following distinction: there are two environmental forces. There is the maternal environmental force, or what I have hitherto described as the 'axis of integration.' And there is the paternal environment force, or what I have hitherto described as the 'axis of regulation.' Psychotic systems, if they are systems at all, are always systems of defence against a latent – or dormant, but nonetheless present – psychosis, and they are for that reason aligned with what Jacques-Alain Miller would name an 'ordinary psychosis'. Put in more common terms, we are dealing with untriggered psychotic systems. The stabilization of a psychotic system (e.g., psychotic systems are always systems of codes or communicative competency) is always fragile the system could break at any moment and dissolve into its environment. This is because a code is always inadequate vis-à-vis its environment, though it attempts to secure itself provisionally through the defence of various 'obstacles' or 'distances' from that environment. During moments of stabilization we can nonetheless see discrete signs of which for Jacques-Alain Miller there are at least three: (1) 'social externality,' (2) 'bodily externality,' and (3) 'subjective externality.'

'Social externality' occurs 'when you have to admit that the subject is unable to assume a social function, when he doesn't fit it [...] when [there is] an 'invisible barrier' [and] 'disconnection'' (Miller, 2015: 155). It is clear that within Luhmann's approach there is a fundamental disconnection of any individual system from its environment, and, from the perspective of that system, there is indeed only its own system as such since any object of the environment, any other foundational code, appears to itself as 'too-much' (as 'noise') which must be channelled into the pre-established framework by way of its central code. The best way to handle this is for the communicative system to carry its own receptacle upon its hip: anything which does not translate into its own code must be tossed into its own waste basket (e.g., according to the political system, if it is not a form of 'power' then it goes into the waste basket of 'powerless'). In this way, all environmental noise is rendered meaningful according to pre-established determinations of a given system. Therefore, the objet petit a does not exist outside of itself as a project, but rather within itself – attached to its hip. 'Bodily externality' as an indicator of psychosis implies that a communicative system must invent a solution to the dislocation of its own body of knowledge. In this case, the Lacanian concept of 'body' is taken broadly: it is the body of knowledge, functioning as a consistency or as a possession, which is of interest.

The subject of psychosis invents a fragile code and inscribes itself upon the body in order to anchor it down. This sometimes occurs quite literally as a tattoo, as rings or jewelry, as hair dye, as fashion/clothing, and so on. In any case, a communicative system anchors its body of codes down through the invention of a mark of its own singularity, and this helps it to distinguish itself from the threatening environmental Other. The code replaces or substitutes the Name-of-the-Father in its relationship to the body (Miller, 2015: 157). Finally, the 'subjective externality' involves an experience of 'emptiness and vagueness' (Miller, 2015: 157). Although this much is clear already from Luhmann's insistence that there are no 'subjects' in his theory, we should nonetheless insist upon the fact that Luhmann's theory attempts to outrun the void which nonetheless compels him (and his systems) toward meaning. For example, the education system must fill 'the void of necessary internal determinations [...] [with] ideals and organization, [with] ideologies and professional politics, but above all by autonomous reflective theories' (Luhmann, 1995: 206). The code of a system is always a mark of its defence against the real void which remains in the waste basket of its own determinations. It is this void which we must bring to the fore.

3. Avoiding the Void

Incidentally, Luhmann discovered a problem of the void in his reading of Talcott Parsons' systems theory. Luhmann claimed that Parsons' social system is grounded upon a primordial and determinative void:

> [W]hen one thus broadens the framework of possible solutions to the problem Parsons's theory poses, one at once opens the theory more powerfully to chance. We can connect this with the 'order from noise principle' of general systems theory. No preordained value consensus is needed; the problem of double contingency (i.e., empty, closed, indeterminable self-reference) draws in chance straightaway, creates sensitivity to chance, and when no value consensus exists, one can thereby invent it. The system emerges etsi no daretur Deus [even if God doesn't exist]. (Luhmann, 1995: 105)

This powerful statement implies that the lack of the paternal signifier – God – does not separate the subject properly in the world of language. As such, 'even if God doesn't exist' there can exist a substitution, a making-do without God, to tranquilize the 'noise' or 'emptiness' of jouissance from the maternal environment. The system should therefore operate upon the void itself – the fact of God not existing – by 'inventing' solutions to manage this jouissance. It is important to distinguish the logic of a code from the logic of a signifier.

Luhmann relates his codes to George Spencer Brown's Laws of Form (1969). According to Brown's logic, there is always a 'marked' and 'unmarked' space of distinction. It is the distinction itself – similar, in effect, to Gottleb Frege's 'judgment stroke' – which implies that something like castration or a paternal signifier exists. However, for Luhmann, the distinction between what is marked and what is unmarked is such that there can be both marked and unmarked within a communicative sphere itself. And, finally, this necessitates an inadequate distinction which must be endlessly navigated by the system. This is what Parsons perhaps meant when he discussed 'boundary maintenance.' Communicative systems are attempts to produce and explore the consequences of pragmatic and self-generated distinctions which are projected into the real environment (rather than internalized once and for all from the symbolic environment). In the final analysis, since the environment itself is a void, it must be made to exist through boundary maintenance.

The communicative system invents for itself an environment which would be a threat to its own code: 'since my own code is love, then, that which I do not understand is not-love.' The environment is rendered 'not-love' though, from the perspective of the environment, this code never actually existed to begin; it was rather as invented as a castration of the code itself (precisely to legitimize the code which didn't anyway exist either). The system constructs a code which mimics the logic of lack and not-lacking, of phi and minus-phi, to substitute for the more radical trauma of lack-lacking or void/hole. For Luhmann, then, the communicative system is ultimately responsible for the function of marking distinctions. This is different from a neurotic system which inherits distinctions made by the environment itself. I return again to my example of American and Indian social bonds to illustrate this point: whereas American traffic is regulated to some extent by external distinctions (red light/green light, stop sign/no stop sign, and so on) the Indian system implicates drivers in their own productions of distinctions, internally. King & Thornhill have explained this logic very well:

> [W]hat is not selected appears as 'the unmarked state' and remains indeterminate or undefined. However, this indeterminate area is not just a nameless void. It is labelled and exists as one side of a 'form' which has been brought into existence through the operation of making a distinction. (King & Thornhill, 2003: 12)

Finally, we can affirm that the communicative system itself endlessly produces its own distinctions within itself in order to produce an environmental Other which is otherwise radically absent. Systems are always self-generated solutions to the problem of trauma, and this is why a love system is always the production of certainty: it produces the partner from the noise of its environment, which it has then convinced itself, according to some internal code, that is 'lovable' or worthy of love. Yet, we should be clear: King & Thornhill's point regarding the unmarked state of the code as not being a 'nameless void' is correct only in that the void itself takes on the function of a name. Thus, it is not a nameless void, but rather a void as the foundation for a name. Thus, the void becomes a prop for the function of a name (the chief function of which is to produce separation from environmental jouissance).

The Luhmannian understanding of a system of communication teaches us that any system interprets its environment through its own internalized epistemological system. The example I have been using is 'politics,' which circulates the codes of 'powerful' and 'powerless.' However, the environment does not exist except through a systemization of love itself. Love is the name that I have given for any attempt at producing a certain distinction in the following way: 'lovable' and 'not-lovable.' For example, a system may communicate: 'I love this woman' or else it may unmark the object of its environment, 'I do not love this woman.' Love is also the name I give to a system's attempt to expand the parameters of its holophrastic system –

even if that system be political or religious in nature. It is in the name of love that politics seeks to expand its certainty, and it is in the name of love that Jews, Christians, Muslims, and Hindus spread the codes of their doctrine. Love is therefore perverse, it is a 'pere-version,' since it is a turning toward a father signifier; in other words, it is a type of boundary mechanism, the results of which shall define the limits of its communicative competency.

These efforts on the part of the system are sure to provoke anxiety in the subject, if indeed one exists. Or, likewise, they are sure to provoke anxiety in the environmental Other – the subject and the environmental Other are the same thing, according to Lacan: S is related fundamentally to the signifier of the lack in the Other, S(~A) – because they signal the existence of a primordial traumatic void. Indeed, the subject is produced only by way of generating a boundary between the subject and the Other. Hernes and Bakken confirm this boundary-seeking behaviour of a system:

> Similar to [Talcott] Parsons, Luhmann defines social systems as being principally boundary-maintaining systems [...] However, [Luhmann's] autopoietic theory differs starkly from this position [because of the] assumption that boundaries can only be drawn from inside the system. [...] Self-reference takes place on the basis of the inside of the boundary, and represents, consequently, closure in relation to the environment. (Hernes & Bakken, 2003: 1519)

This operational closure has led Weick to claim that for Luhmann '[t]he 'outside' or 'external' world cannot be known. The outside is a void, there is only inside' (Weick, 1977: 273). Luhmann's systems are meant to describe the relative stabilization of psychosis through the circulation of holophrastic does within a delusional mode of intra-subjectivity to produce an environment (rather than an inter-subjective model which interacts with its environment).

Luhmann's sociological approach to the topic of love restricts its focus to the 'symbolic medium of communication' without recognizing that there is also an ontological dimension to love. Rumi reportedly wrote that 'love is not an emotion, it is your very existence.' Love's ontological dimension is grounded in the Lacanian notion of sex, except that it is more: it is the acceptance of the ontological impossibility of sex as lack-in-being, and the sharing of that lack so that it might endure. The ontological dimension of love exists as the auto-poietic epistemological limitation to meaning and communication, but also as the possibility of finding there within the void of the lack-of-being codes or words which might express that traumatic gap. In this way, love is not only a communicative system that strives for legitimacy and hegemony against its real environment, but it is also, and more essentially, a sustained engagement with the hole or lack. To love is to communicate what one doesn't mean, which is, in other words, to assume lack as the foundation for any distinction and as the source of its primordial trauma and destruction. Love is to assume the risk that the system might destroy itself – but it is also more than that, it is itself the fall of a system into the depth of its unmarked space. Politics has love at is very foundation: the code 'powerful' is related fundamentally to the phallus and it marks a distinction against the hole of castration, or 'powerless.' Politics is the truth of the system in the same way that Lacan once claimed that politics is unconscious.

Politicians must be distinguished from revolutionaries. Whereas the politician is the one who operates by attempting to broaden an underlying epistemological code of power, revolutionaries operate upon the hole itself by recognizing within the political sphere the fact of a hole which separates the subject from the intensity of unrestrained economic drives. Politics must therefore also be the name for any defence mounted by groups against the jouissance of their individual liberty. Alain Badiou famously attempted to work through Lacan's claim (which was itself a reformulation of Freud's claim) that philosophy and metaphysics 'plugs the hole' of politics (see Badiou, 2013). We might presume a simple typology: political secularism is the name for that system which separates religion from the jouissance of economic liberty. Islam, therefore, is a system, by most accounts, that does not consist of this separation. The Western phrase 'political Islam' is a contradiction in terms. The Western political system has too much interpreted its environment according to its own established codes of conduct. To understand the role of the political within Islam is to fall in love with other points of view. The battle of discourses or systems – politics versus religion, in this case – is nothing of the sort: it is first of all a battle that each system has with its own unmarked space of distinction. For example, only Christianity permits the circulation of codes of politics (e.g., secularism – since, in my reading, politics can only exist as secular), since Christianity is a system of boundary-maintenance. Islam, however, as a system of communication, remains a distinctively religious discourse without its consequent mutation into political discourse. To be a revolutionary within Islam therefore has no meaning, or else it requires us to rethink its meaning in terms of love.

Finally, all of this implies that at the base of communicative systems is not a so-called battle of discourses, such as those outlined by Michel Foucault, whereby politics struggles alongside psychiatry which struggles alongside religion, and so on. Not at all! I begin rather with the presumption that religious social bonds are a major factor in understanding the development of communicative systems and that they may be somewhere close to the foundation of all discursive realities. Thus, my corrective is precisely similar in form to the one made so many decades ago by Max Weber. Weber's response to Karl Marx, in his The Protestant Ethic and the Spirit of Capitalism (2009 [1905]), was the following: if capitalism embodies the contradictions of feudalism and all other preceding political-economic realities then why have so many feudal systems not transformed directly into capitalism? His answer, of course, was that religious systems are somehow at the base and serve as a major factor in these developments. In particular, Calvinism and Protestantism are key features which have given rise to capitalism. Weber famously wrote: '[i]n order that a manner of life well adapted to the peculiarities of capitalism [...] could come to dominate others, it had to originate somewhere, and not in isolated individuals alone, but as a way of life common to the whole groups of man' (Weber, 1905). What we thus find through Weber is an adequate response to the materialist presumptions of Marx: political economic reality is based upon sociological ideational content, or, put another way, the religious-spirit is a political-economic bone.

Politics consists always of a symbolic hole which separates and provides a space for the economic subject to desire liberty, whereby liberty is simply the subjective desire to return to the intensity of his economic or religious bond. Luhmann is therefore incorrect to claim that politics is defined by the code of 'power' for two reasons: first, 'power' is the code of love, and love is fundamental, and; second, what is at stake in politics is not power but rather the maintenance of a distance or void which must be maintained (and whose content is only of secondary significance). No wonder the French consider their secularist politics as 'pure,' since, in effect, it is pure! The French are fanatically secularist because their boundaries must be maintained and defended at all costs, they must remain pure of environmental contaminants. We see the movement toward a purist and fundamentalist secularism also within the United States under the Trump administration (e.g., the wall, immigration crack-down, etc.). The structures of fascism are therefore already in place within the systemic make-up of our communicative constitution. The revolutionary perspective is therefore to find within the secularist attitude a hole which is no longer merely symbolic and political, but one which may be assumed as the foundation of subjectivity itself, the foundation upon which certainty may be established as the formation of a universal bond such as that found in the Islamic ummah. In this way, we see that the true opposition today is between fascism and revolution, demonstrating very well why for Walter Benjamin 'every fascism falls on the heels of a failed revolution.'

The subject emerges within Islam not through the space of a political hole but rather through the broadening of a shared certainty, that is, through the extension of basic presuppositions and convictions. Structurally speaking, there can be no political Islam. Yet, for Christianity, there is an insistence upon a moveable line of distinction: 'render unto Caesar the things that are Caesar's; and to God the things that are God's' (Matthew, 22:21). We therefore have a choice of two modalities of love among Christians or Muslims. The Christians love their neighbours, in obedience to the second great commandment, but always precisely from a distance and difference – they therefore love their neighbours as themselves, in their own image, and through the renewal of their code's fundamental legitimacy. On the other hand, the Muslims love through commonalities with all religions (and through a subtraction of differences), in obedience to their commandment to love by coming to common terms with one another. In other words, the Jews love from the particularity of their own system, the Christians love from the position of a neighbour, and the Muslims love without boundaries or distinction. These three possibilities – indeed, there are more than only these three – open up as three structural possibilities of love.

Love is not simply one of the many communicative spheres of competency, with its own independent code, but rather the limitless dimension of communication as such. It is the endurance of the void which sustains speech, and that which gives rise to communicative codes as such. Bracha L. Ettinger refers to a process of 'communicaring' which involves the sharing of the trauma of the primordial void – of the real, or of hole – with another through the 'transport-station of beauty.' This, it seems to me, is the crux of her beautiful definition of love. Love, for Ettinger, is always a communicative gesture that operates not through the symbolic but rather through the aesthetics of the 'sign,' or what I have been naming a 'code.' Indeed, recently she invented the following 'formula:' 'trauma is truth of love in beauty.' My interpretation is this formula is as follows: the real of trauma constitutes an imaginary substitute for symbolic truth, and this is the only and ever-present foundation of intersubjective exchange through the invention of a beautiful self-referential code. Beauty is therefore linked to being-with since it is only in the real that traumatic being-with is possible.

Ettinger's concept of 'wit(h)nessing' helps us to understand how the primordial traumatic 'fall,' that fall into the void which grounds any system, finds its witness in love. Love requires this 'wit(h)nessing' or else it is nothing. Alain Badiou has also insisted upon this 'with' when he defined love as a 'two scene.' Put another way, love requires that it be situated in time, beyond the occurrence of the traumatic event, through the guarantee of another person, to establish an impossible zone of intersubjectivity. Alain Badiou's theory of the 'two scene' of love demonstrates that it is only by passing through two that love can sustain itself. Minimally, there must be two people, or, put another way, there must be a system which sees within itself the split which separates its code from its underlying void, its conscious intention from its unconscious determinations. Love has no meaning without this moment of suspension in time. It is the moment of passience, the moment of traumatic patience which permits it to endure within the pain of time's distance. For Badiou (2012), it is this 'two scene' which opens up the space for the mutual exploration of unconscious determinations, such that a retroactive truth for the inherent and unnameable trauma may be proposed: 'in the name of love, … we were always meant to be.' The process of generating a name function, that is, a code of one's certain, is important.

If 'trauma is truth of love in beauty' then we can claim also that the eventual occurrence is retroactively established by the beautiful, patient, and enduring love of the 'two scene.' This is why love, as a sharing of beautiful trauma, is 'impossible to not share' (Ettinger, 2001). It is only by opening up the communicative bubble to the void that a linkage might be established beyond the self-referential codes. Ettinger writes that:

> [T]he desire to join-in-difference and differentiate-in-co-emerging with the Other doesn't promise any peace and harmony, because joining is first of all joining with-in the other's trauma that echoes backwards to my archaic traumas: joining the other matrixially is always joining the m/Other and risking a mental fragmentation and vulnerability. (Ettinger, 2001: 107-8)

We cannot help but not participate in the fall of love, and we cannot help but be tempted to endless share this experience with others. Just as the real is that which never steps not being written by the symbolic order, so too is love the experience which never stops not being experienced as traumatic. Love must be said to be rooted in some ontological space, in some space akin to the real unconscious. It is the real unconscious which

Luhmann's system retains but nonetheless a-voids. For Ettinger, a primordial connection with the real mother persists within any system, so that there is always the possibility of intersubjectivity. But this intersubjective possibility is not reducible to that which has been popularly accepted from Habermas's theory. Jurgen Habermas reduces intersubjectivity also to a communicative gesture but for him it can only be guaranteed by the erection of a transcendental system of symbolic rules, so-called the 'ideal speech situation.' This is a very dangerous game: the appeal to traditional external symbolic systems is also a plea to return to the symbolic and paternal authority of the past. It is only through the traumatic real that a link might be established beyond the self-referential environment toward a real environment. The system must fall, it must see within its own babbling, within its own miscommunication, within the unmarked space outside of its code's authority, the truth of its love.

4. Talcott Parsons and Pragmatic Sociology

For Luhmann, as well as Parsons before him, underlying personality systems are based upon relationships among egos (which are themselves organized and consistent systems). In other words, ego is a principle of rendering, a principle of consistency, and it was a part of Lacan's genius to have argued persuasively about this. Luhmann refused to give up on the Parsonsian claim that systems are always made up of systems and are therefore always submerged within other systems. A system is therefore always also a system of systems. This position of schizophrenic multiplicity is not unlike that of Gilles Deleuze and his followers. This explains why Parsons' reading of Freud always passed through the American pragmatists and the object-relations theorists/clinicians and avoided, indeed rejected, theories of the Freudian 'unconscious' and 'drives.' A case could be made that pragmatic sociology and philosophy is more aligned with the schizophrenia model proposed by Deleuze. Like the vast majority of American sociologists, Parsons rejected the Freudian drives and unconscious because of its supposed fixation upon biological determinations. But Parsons was also one of relatively few American sociologists to have explored Freudian theory and technique with any serious consideration. Indeed, he trained at the Boston Psychoanalytic Institute under Grete Bibring in 1946, and he seemed to have frequented clinical gatherings.

The problem with Parsons' approach was that he subsumed the Freudian insights to a relatively discrete sub-system, the 'personality system.' Symbolic interactionist and psychoanalytic notions were present but always in compacted form, always reduced to lower powers determined by those higher and transcendental social and cultural systems. Parsons' lower systems, the 'behavioural' and 'personality' systems, provided the resources for the overarching system while the aforementioned higher systems harnessed those resources and channeled them through the imperatives of 'pattern maintenance' and 'integration.' In support of this claim, Davenport wrote that '[m]ore than anything else [...] Parsons relied upon [...] psychoanalytic theory for the personality level of his theory of action' (Davenport, 1966: 275). Parsons ignored what was most Freudian about Freudian theory, focusing only on what could be possessed or harnessed by the cultural system: a theory of object-relations or personality systems grounded in the material resources of the behavioural system. Hence, there, in the behavioural system, is the 'stuff' of a-voidance: its function is to adapt to the real environment through extraction of the resources. This is the origin of the Luhmannian 'code.'

Parsons was motivated to demonstrate the social applicability of Freud's discovery and to do so he was forced to ignore the real Freud. Parsons wrote:

> The primary emphasis in interpreting Freud's work – at least in the United States – has tended to be on the power of the individual's instinctual needs and the deleterious effects of their frustration. [...] The consequence of such a trend is to interpret Freud as a psychologist who brought psychology closer to the biological sciences, and to suggest the relative unimportance of society and

culture, except as these constitute agencies of the undesirable frustration of man's instinctual needs. (Parsons, [1958] 2016: 321)

Yet, what if the true Freudian discovery was not the 'individual psychology' but rather the real stratum associated with the emergence of society and culture? The problem was once again that Parsons could not conceive of a non-biological and hence non-psychological Freudian 'real' associated with the embodied drives. He could not foresee within Freud's work the determinations of a real which would contribute not only to the system's inherent frustration but also to the very formation of a social or systemic bond. And American sociologists persist in their interpretation of the biological instincts or drives in Freud's work, finding therein a naïve biological position that has been unpalatable for social science and humanities scholars steeped in the linguistic turn (see Seidman, 2014). Parsons therefore misses what is most real in Freud's work: Freud was not most interested in affirming the priority the 'object' or the 'ego' but rather in the agency of 'lack.' Lack, as in, lack of object,' that is, in the real of 'castration anxiety' is determinative for the subject. Lacan explained:

> [W]e cannot pose the problem of the object relation correctly unless we begin with a certain framework that must be considered as fundamental. [...] This framework, or the first of these frameworks, is that in the human world, the lack of the object provides the structure as well as the beginning of objectal [systemic] organization. (Lacan, 2018: 53)

Instead of focusing on the real frustrations of individuals – frustrations of ego, image, possession – the object-relations theorists, and, by implication this includes also Parsons and Luhmann, seemed to be interested in an imaginary mode of stabilization through the consistency and repetition of codes. The paradox is therefore that Parsons did not want to engage with the real frustrations in Freudian theory. He was doom therefore to reproduce them in his own project, as a return of the repressed: a system is always threatened by its environment and so must tirelessly persist in its boundary-maintenance.

Thus, a system can never relax. Its drives are feral drives.

In every case, Luhmann, like Parsons before him, presumed that society is based upon relationships among its constituent parts and that systems are derived from systems and that there are multiplicities of atomistic ones all the way down (Luhmann, 1998: 12, 13). Thus, a system is always a collection of ones-all-alone, forever in isolation, forever circulating the codes of its own internal egoistic narcissism to protect itself against the traumatizing and threatening real of its environment. Jacques-Alain Miller claimed that this is the urgency with which the psychoanalyst must respond in the twenty-first century. Maria Cristina Aguirre summarizes the Millerian teaching:

> Following Lacan's proposition in his last teachings, what is at stake in the practice of psychoanalysis today is to find, case by case, the particular way a subject can find an exit from the trap of narcissism with his own resources – imaginary, symbolic, or real – by organizing a link to the Other, in the era of the One All Alone. (Aguirre, 2018)

The contemporary Lacanian orientation begins from a radically different point of departure than the system-all-alone with its one-code-all-alone: any system, any ego, is based always upon a lack-of-relation. We should therefore undermine the lowest level of the system which begins, according to Luhmann, from its 'real assets' (Luhmann, 1998: 10), since love is not at all an asset that one can give. For example, Luhmann claimed that truth obtains its 'real assets' from perception, love from sexuality, money from elementary needs, and power from force (Luhmann, 1998: 10). The problem is first of all with the 'asset' which is not for Luhmann real enough. From what system does one determine whether or not one has an asset? Moreover, is 'having' (an asset) itself a systemic foundational code? Truth does not obtain its asset from the resources of perception any more than Eurydice is obtained through the phallic gaze. Indeed, the truth of Orpheus is that the God's deceived him precisely to expose the truth of the inadequacy of the phallic gaze / perception. Next, the claim that love obtains its assets from sexuality relies upon a resource-based understanding of libido as quantity and the drives while ignoring the dimension of sex as an inherent void or stumbling-block (for more on this position of sex as void see Zupančič, 2017; also see Žižek, 2019).

Marx already disrupted the popular notion that money is based upon 'needs' (or, similarly, 'having' or 'assets') when he wrote:

> Man becomes even poorer as his need for money becomes ever greater[…].The power of his money declines in inverse proportion to the increase in the volume of production: that is, his neediness grows as the power of money increases. The need for money is therefore the true need produced by the economic system, and it is the only need which the latter produces. (Marx, 1844)

We can see once again that love, as an obstacle to virility and power, is operating within Marx's economic work. Marx discovered that money produces its own need as well as its own limitation precisely as wealth and illusions of power increase. It is not that an economy is based upon needs but rather that needs are themselves produced as semblance as a condition of the economic system itself. Thus, the behavioural system is itself subservient to the higher systems in a much more insidious way than we typically believe.

Finally, Luhmann claimed that power has its resource in 'force.' The imaginary phallus substitutes for the minus-phi of castration, and this is the real source of power. He believes that the political system's code of 'powerful' marks itself against 'powerless' without recognizing that it is a defence against precisely the inverse: the fear of 'powerlessness' is what gives rise to any attempt at 'power.' Yet, already, with the unmarked code of powerlessness – as the symbolic unconscious of a system – there is a formation against the navel or hole which swallows both marked and unmarked codes. Lacan said the following: 'the One […] is symbolized by the imaginary function that incarnates powerlessness, in other words, by the phallus […]. In psychoanalysis it is a matter of raising powerlessness to logical impossibility' (Lacan, 2018b: 219). Systems displace their innate 'powerlessness' outward into the environment from via the code as a technique against the real push of the unconscious. The unmarked 'powerlessness' cannot exist anywhere else except already within the symbolic unconscious of a narcissistic system: it is the Other which forms the backdrop of every communicative gesture. Does this not also explain why sadism and masochism are often found within the same system, whereby the one is the hidden yet displaced truth of the other? Lacan claimed that 'sadism is merely the disavowal of masochism,' since the sadist rejects the experience of castration anxiety (minus-phi) and so forces the environment to bear that anxiety instead (Lacan, 1977: 186).

Among the many remaining confusions within Luhmann's work, there is the repeated one that love obtains its resources from sexuality when in fact it is sexuality which obtains its status as a resource precisely via the conduit of love: love is radically without foundation in sexuality since its functional imperative is to compensate for the traumatic hole of sex. It is sex which is without marking, even within the unmarked side of the code! Therefore, to truly fall in love with systems theory, or to fall in love as a systems theorist, is to begin a number of productive mis-readings of Luhmann's systems theory of love. Let us begin with his theory of functional difference. His claim that systems become functionally differentiated from themselves implies that each system relinquishes that which it finds inconsistent with itself. For example, in medieval times, though religion was a dominant hegemonic system, it gave rise to other distinct systems such as education, law, and health, which distinguished themselves from the originating system on the basis of a new code. We might expect that systems become increasingly differentiated in time, yet, nonetheless, certain systems become 'functionally primary.' But today, through increasing fragmentation and the proliferation of distinctive codes, we live in a time of the loss of love: system theory is evidence enough of the loss of love, since it is a discourse of the One-All-Alone. In place of love, there is only the certainty of a code (to be distinguished from the code of certainty).

Today we also have the greatest chance to experience love. Perhaps love is the communicative sphere par excellence. The holophrastic zone of delusional productions can today obtain a certainty from the sharing of its hole – beyond the unmarked space of distinction – through a process of what Bracha L. Ettinger refers to as 'communicaring' (Ettinger, 2001). This co-autopoeitic or 'co-poeitic' activity (Ettiner's words) is the only possibility of re-attaching to our environment (which anyway never leaves us), the only possibility of communal exchange, the only manner of stabilization; it is the beauty of what Ettinger names 'traumatic love' as the ontological space opened up by the lack-of-being. Within psychotic communicative bubbles there is no longer any subject, but only a deafening and threatening environment noise which has emerged as a consequence of symbolic foreclosure: when the symbolic is foreclosed, it re-emerges in the real of its environment.

IV

Love Letters

1. To Love is to be Sick

There have been four major claims made in this book. The first two claims concern today's major threat to love: the fact of its possible foreclosure. This means that it is increasingly unlikely for an individual to fall in love unless that new commitment functions primarily to supplement one's career aspirations, spiritual journey, pursuit of happiness, expansion and consolidation of pre-existing friendship networks, and so on. The individual in America is invited to abandon love because it can only distract him from his membership into an atomistic and lonely community. Today's individuals are all alone in their life goals, and their pursuits are marked by the goals of 'self-care.' Love often appears to each individual as a problematic dogma, or, rather, an addiction that must be cured. The lover is considered sick by his friends, colleagues, and family because he is willing to give up on all of his future gains, he is willing to risk his mental and physical health, and he is willing to give up on what he has (or on what he could possibly have later) in order to fundamentally reorient himself around the lover. The profound risk of love does not promise him a return.

Today's wannabe lovers treat their relationships as if they were subjected to the same laws that one would find defining the sorts of behaviours occurring within investment firms. The loved one must satisfy all of the lovers pre-existing criteria, including demographic criteria, life goals, and so on. In other words, the relationship is reduced, if possible, to the status of a low risk investment, effectively destroying the very experience that one aimed to inaugurate: passion. Thus, love is lost from the very beginning, and today's lovers inhabit this cold new world. Yet, the risk of love's foreclosure can be rectified through the processes of invention: against immense societal pressures to do otherwise, the subject must invent for himself a new mode of loving through certainty. In this way, love itself could be a solution to its own foreclosure: to love is to reject the world of commodification, the world of investments, and so on. In other words, to love is to exit the capitalist discourse and to occupy the position of the Saint. The Saint, in this case, is the one who renders himself useless to the pragmatic society of circulating commodities; he is the one who, like Joker in Todd Phillip's new film, invents for himself a mode of being and laughs at it all.

Incidentally, are we not prepared to admit that Joker was a Saint? Daniel Tutt argued the following:

> The Joker thus abandons the super-egoic function he had identified with [one of his father substitutes] and transposes a new superego identification with the political uprising in Gotham [...] Although he insisted [...] that he is not 'political,' the Joker becomes a newly born political figure after ridding himself of the father of the imaginary and symbolic. (Tutt, 2019)

It is not my intention to provide a summary of comprehensive commentary on the film Joker, but I do want to make some amendments and develop Daniel Tutt's argument a bit further. My own position is that Joker is not a political film. Neither is it a revolutionary film, as some have maintained – and, also, it is not at all an 'alt-right' film, since, by making this claim, we end up reproducing a fundamental aporia which I have already commented upon (and which was picked up by Slavoj Žižek in our reading of the film Black Panther, namely that alt-right and ultra left commentary ended up becoming strikingly similar). Indeed, films today have a 'platform' logic in their ideological function: the ambiguous nature of the film strikes chords with a wide variety of cultural critics and satisfies absolutely opposing political agendas. Thus, I maintain only that the film is about subjective transformation, and that it is here that we might glean some insight.

I propose that we interpret the film by reading it alongside an important transcript of a talk that Jacques-Alain Miller gave in Milan, Two Intuitions in Milan (2002). At this time Miller was exploring a fundamental question of the relationship of the unconscious to politics – it is a topic that has become once again important in recent years for the World Association of Psychoanalysis – and we have the statement 'unconscious is politics.' We should situate this statement. Let us begin with the classical Lacanian/Freudian understanding of the unconscious. The unconscious is fundamentally related to its symbolic anchoring point, the name of the father, which provides it with the possibility of discourse. Finally, it is discourse which constitutes a social bond. (Love, we might claim, is a discourse situated at the impossibility of sex.) Miller concludes that the unconscious therefore implies a connection in some sense to society and to the city:

> The definition of the unconscious by politics goes very deep in Lacan's teaching. 'The unconscious is politics' is a development of 'the unconscious is the discourse of the Other.' This link to the Other, intrinsic to the unconscious, is what inspires from the outset Lacan's teaching. This is also true when it is pointed out that the Other is divided and does not exist as One. (Miller, 2002)

The problem is that the contemporary period is marked by a decline in the symbolic efficiency of the paternal function, the loss of the virility of the name of the father. Thus, there are problems with proper names. Tutt correctly diagnosed the fact that the film is situated within the general topic of the problem of the loss of the function of proper names and the decline of the father's role. But we should also notice that the film is named 'Joker' and not 'the Joker.' The latter proper name was prevalent in earlier discussions of the character: he was often referred to as the Joker. But great care was given to avoid that in the current film. We witness the removal of the definite article.

We should also notice that Joker does not laugh when the others are laughing in the film. He does not laugh as a consequence of his participation in a social group. He laughs according to his own timing, and his jokes are self-referential and one-liners. He does not feel inclined to explain the joke, nor does he care much if the other 'gets' the message of the joke. Why? It is clear that Joker does not have an Other, such that he is forced, in some sense, to try to invent one. Without this Other there can be no politics. There is no politics for the psychotic subject since politics consists precisely in the distanciation of economic jouissance, and no such distanciation yet existed for Joker. The city as Other also ceases to exist for Joker, since he remains delinked from Gotham. Like many individuals in Gotham city, they view the city as if it were on fire. It is on fire because its function is no longer operational. Miller writes on the city, the following:

> The city does not exist. [...] Today, we no longer have 'the City.' It is imaginary. We hear it as a metaphor for politics, but [...] politics is not developed in the form of the City. The City is a residue nostalgia, it is also imaginary in the sense that we look for it today to find it in the television. (Miller, 2002)

The subject is therefore increasingly delinked from the social bond, from politics, from the city, from the unconscious itself, and, indeed, from discourse. There is only for him 'a discourse which is not one,' a discourse of semblance, the capitalist discourse. Capitalist discourse is different from the traditional four discourses in Lacanian thought – that of Master, University, Hysteria, and Analyst – because it brings with it a greater emphasis on the drives. These drives are the place of jouissance, and it is jouissance – excessive stimulation – which is put on display in Joker. Miller claims that:

> [The] level of the drive, which, unlike desire, is not intrinsically articulated to a defence, is the level to which Lacan has attributed the property 'the subject is always happy,' ... always happy ... on the level of the drive that is, the only question

being that of the mode of satisfaction, pleasurable, painful, etc., while axiomatically, the drive is always satisfied. (Miller, 2002)

Is this not the lesson of Joker, who demonstrates so obviously the 'always happy' push of the drive through his bloody smile? Joker is not the typical hysterical or obsessional subject who simply wishes to get revenge on a father figure or else to be loved by him. He is rather a subject for whom these father figures have never truly existed except through the imaginary, so that, finally, he was pushed, endlessly, to invent substitute father figures from whom he might learn how to be a proper subject. It was from them that he sought to make a name for himself. His proximity to his mother demonstrates to us the failure of the father's function: there he was in her bed, and, at another time there he is without any qualms bathing her naked body.

After his mother's death, Joker climbs into a refrigerator and closes it. This womb-like structure swallows him entirely. This was a clear pathological repetition of the mother's presence, an intention to reproduce the structure which compelled his psychosis. But this scene also hints at the notorious 'refrigerator mother' theory of autism by Leo Kanner and Bruno Bettelheim. The claim was that in autism and schizophrenia – both are types of psychosis – there are the following dynamics: a cold mother who exhibits signs of what we today call depression and a withdrawn father who refuses to intervene as a law-maker in the life of the child. The Lacanian and Kleinian position is not quite as literal but finds nonetheless some truth in this controversial position: Joker's object-relations were such that the objects of the world devour him completely, thereby removing any possibility for the installation of lack. His imaginary father figures promise to rescue him from this nightmare but endlessly fail.

Miller claims that the role of the father has changed:

It is easy to see what still attaches psychoanalysis to the myth of the father, and to see that society, in the process of modification at this epoch of globalization, has ceased to live under the reign of the father. Why not say it in our own language, the structure of the all has given way to that of the not-all: the structure of the not-all implies precisely that there be nothing left that serves as a barrier. (Miller, 2002)

It seems to me that this opens up the possibility that the film is not only about psychosis but also about capitalist discourse in relation to psychosis. There is no longer a barrier because there is no longer a father. Consequently, there is no longer a social bond. Yet, at one point in the film, does Joker not discover, precisely through the certainty of his delusion, a place for himself, paradoxically, within the social bond? There he stands atop of a car looking endlessly at his own face in the crowd. His social bond – the one he never wanted – was constructed paradoxically through the narcissism of his own delusion.

The only way out of capitalist discourse was therefore for Joker to invent a name for himself. Joker is the name of his symptom, just as for Rat Man and Wolf Man the symptom elevated itself to the status of something like a proper name (or, to put it more correctly, it is a name as prop). Joker is that which was most rejected elevated to the status of acceptance. Joker was the name of his dismissal by imaginary father figures, it was the very mark of the foreclosure of the name of the father, and it was, finally, the name of that which he denied forcefully: laughter, which, as jouissance, once caused him so much pain now rings throughout the land freely. In adopting this name, he rendered himself completely useless for his environment. He became the void of the joke which once defined his system (no longer 'funny' or 'not funny'):

Murray Franklin: Let me get this straight, you think that killing those guys is funny?

Arthur Fleck: I do, and I'm tired of pretending it's not. Comedy is subjective, Murray. Isn't that what they say? All of you, the system that knows so much, you decide what's right or wrong. The same way that you decide what's funny or not.

Joker is here demonstrating that he was up against the communicative system of Arthur Fleck. When he claims that 'all of you, the system […] decide what's […] funny or not' he is subverting the code of Arthur Fleck himself, which interprets his environment in precisely that way. Yet, the subjective transformation into Joker refuses this binary code and launches forth through holophrastic jouissance:

Psychiatrist: What's so funny? Do you want to tell it to me?

Joker: You wouldn't get it.

Joker's laugh throughout the early part of the film demonstrated a level of jouissance, of pain and pleasure at the same time, of crying and smiling at the same time. Finally, during the last part of the film, after his subjective transformation, after killing his mother and becoming himself the father he lacked, he laughed authentically. He laughed, finally, as a mode of organizing his jouissance. At this moment, Joker finally became a Saint.

In any case, a preliminary opposition now appears: there is the subject's refusal to fall in love (whereby love involves 'separation' from the various preordained objects of culture, or else it involves 'jouissance management'), and there are the subject's feelings of delusional certainty. It is clear that the latter position has become exceptional within contemporary American capitalist society. A second opposition concerns the communication or transferability of love. Love, understood as a major threat to any communicative system (as well as the foundation thereof), is radically without boundary. There is an infiniteness to love that produces an 'oceanic feeling,' a feeling often described in the experiences of mystics and found also in the experience described by Freud's mystical companion at the beginning of Civilization and Its Discontents. If at one time this 'oceanic feeling' was thought by Freud to be defined by a desire to return to some mythical primordial harmony with the maternal Other, then today it seems to function as an overwhelming experience that must be avoided at all costs. Thus, boundarylessness is threatening when it is confronted directly without the 'gap' of desire; it involves an overwhelming proximity of jouissance. This traumatic jouissance might be avoided through narcissistic processes of communicative self-referentiality inherent to any system's goal of boundary maintenance. In this case, there is an opposition between the traumatic inability to produce a boundary for the experience of love (its 'boundarylessness') and the constant defensive negotiation of boundaries (its technique of 'boundary negotiation'). These twin oppositions, 'foreclosure' and 'certainty,' 'boundarylessness' and 'boundary negotiation,' might be aligned with the capitalist's discourse, as in the diagram below:

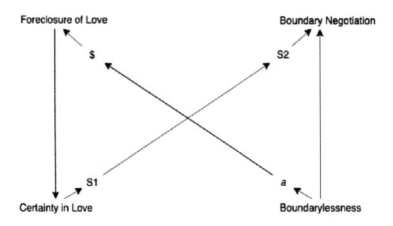

The subject, $, begins in traumatic destitution, swallowed by an overwhelming experience of jouissance. The subject urgently demands a fix, S1. This, in turn, gives rise to a code from which there might be derived a body of signifiers, S2. This body of signifiers remains nonetheless anchored to the 'fix,' until, that is, the process repeats after its initial completion. Put another way, the lover locates in the woman an S1 according to which be begins to derive a body of knowledge concerning his love for her. The lover must always elaborate the consequences of his encounter with the woman and he does so by forming a couple – a 'two' – with the body of meaning, S2. His code, S1, then, forms a social link with his meaning, S2. This couple of S1-S2 will be important for the provisional and fleeting formation of a social bond, it will be a bond that offers some remedy to the trauma which underpins his everyday existence.

Perhaps this is one way to read Alain Badiou's celebrated theory of the 'love event.' The subject, touched by the love event, discovers therein a 'mark' or a 'trace' as semblance of the impossibility which grounds their union, and this compels the lover to invent a code as a way to suture himself to the new possibility in a world that resists saying it. The lover remains in fidelity to that love event by exploring its inherent consequences and possibility, and by working through and inventing a new body of signifiers that compete with and might be increasingly broadened (despite the pressures of the world which attempt to deny it, and which refuse to understand it). Alain Badiou put it like this:

> There is a trace of the [love] event itself. The name exists as a trace of the event. We name the sayable of the event as a trace immanent to the event. It is the fact of the event, but it is not the event itself because the event disappears. But there is a trace. [...] The trace is not inscribed in the common language. All events bring with them linguistic invention. (Badiou, 2012: 85-6)

We can see in this passage the fact of there being a novelty in the expression of a love according to which a love event says something new in a world which hasn't yet established the mode of listening capable of incorporating the new utterances. We might even say that there is no common language for love. Love is always at odds with the world which attempts to give expression to it from without, but the lover sustains himself through the militant conviction that whatever the world says about his love – 'that's not it!' According to the vectorization: from the real of subjective destitution, $, a proper name somehow emerges all alone, S1, and this is an event of pure invention from the real itself. I want to remark for a moment upon the interesting duality of the words 'event' and 'invent,' both sharing the root 'vent' (from venire, meaning 'to come') but both having opposing prefixes: 'in-,' implying 'into' and 'e-' implying 'out of.' In other words, when it comes to the real, there is a 'push' which is a force coming from within the real, and then, by some miracle, there is a mode of invention whereby the subject pulls some meaning out of there where the push was occurring. An invention is made possible by the event of the real.

And this is what gives rise to a body, S2, which is, for Alain Badiou, 'an organically closed set of material traces' (Badiou, 2006). Badiou writes that:

> [A body of] truth presupposes an organically closed set of material traces, traces that refer not to the empirical uses of [an external] world, but to a frontal change. A change which has affected (at least) one object of this world. We could thus say that the trace presupposes that every [body of] truth is the trace of an event. (Badiou, 2006)

Any body of knowledge is anchored fundamentally to the invented code produced from the event of the real. This implies that the subject is retroactively determined as a consequence of his own mode of invention. Thus, it is as if there is something within the real which pushes itself to give birth to a desiring subject. In any case, Badiou discusses an event as the emergence of a 'new possible repetition' irreducible to previously established environmental repetitions. The system of love produces for itself a desire to endlessly reaffirm, repeat, or else reinvent the name of its encounter via the body of its knowledge. The name that Badiou proposes for this repetition is 'fidelity.' When one has fidelity in love then there is an operation of time or an endurance of the code against the tremendous pressure of an environment which seeks endlessly and without fail to once again swallow the subject and destroy its invention. No wonder those who fall passionately in love today are chastised by their colleagues, friends, and family to end the relationship on account of their naïve infatuation. Lovers today are charged with being addicted not to drugs but to their potential partners! Yet, this is also the promise of love today: addiction is sometimes a mode of stabilization by way of which the subject makes-do with his trauma.

We should therefore be careful in presuming always that capitalist discourse – or, for that matter, capitalism – is inherently problematic. It is even possible that capitalist discourse gives rise to the possibility of subjectivity and desire (however fleeting it may be) within an age of generalized psychosis. Stijn Vanheule has argued that capitalist discourse could possibly function as a technique of 'jouissance management' and 'social bonding' for psychotic subjects:

> [I]n the case of neurosis, the discourse of the capitalist functions as an attempt to ignore the sexual non-rapport and the dimension of the unconscious. Psychosis, by contrast, is marked by an a priori exclusion from discourse. In that case, consumerist ways of relating to the other might offer a semblance, and thus the possibility of inventing a mode of relating to the other. (Vanheule, 2016: 1)

We should not take capitalist discourse as the exclusive name for a particular political-economic relationship. Capitalist discourse exists also (and perhaps even more so) within counter-cultural and anti-capitalist communities. Capitalist discourse seems to be the most prevalent structure responsible for today's so-called 'newest symptoms,' symptoms which include self-harm, eating disorders, attention deficit disorder, depression, addiction, and so on. Once again, Vanheule explains:

> From a clinical perspective, [there has been a] shift [...] to a capitalist discourse [...] evidenced in certain changes in contemporary psychopathology, and [this] has brought about much discussion among Lacanians regarding what they call contemporary symptoms. Such symptoms, including addiction, panic or borderline states of functioning, are not thought of as metaphorical constructions that need deciphering but as subjective expression of, and reactions to, overwhelming surplus jouissance. (Vanheule, 2016: 9)

Similarly, the Lacanian 'university discourse' was never supposed to exclusively describe those social bonds within academia. University discourse could have very well been found in capitalist relations during the late part of the twentieth century (see Fink, 1995: 132). Capitalist discourse was also never meant to exempt supposedly 'non-capitalist' situations such as activist communities or spaces, social movements, and so on. Here, the situation is much more complicated. The university today is one of the primary sites for the expansion and perpetuation

101

of capitalist discourse since the neo-liberal institution compels students to demand prefabricated chunks of knowledge in the form of course modules, lists, concepts/definitions, etc., which are to be delivered in quick bursts and then abruptly forgotten (Rousselle, 2019). Indeed, within the American university today courses are frequently designed so as to lead the student from topic to topic without the requisite consistency of there being an overarching universal commitment. Consistency in university discourse would have traditionally been built upon established knowledge (whereby the goal was to make 'yet another' original contribution to the body of knowledge: the 'unknown' was to be made consistent with what was already known).

It is important for today's anti-capitalist professors to refuse these demands. The student who demands a module or a slide is today doing nothing more than demanding a 'quick fix,' and then, rather than cutting through or offering an alternative to capitalist discourse, (s)he finds him or herself perfectly aligned within it. The professor who interrupts this demand by refusing the temptation to capsulize knowledge provokes in the student and in the institution an anxiety which was nonetheless already present, an anxiety against which the capsulized education was attempting to outrun. The professor opens up the space of the impossible event and thereby teaches out of love. Today's professors who teach out of love are not only a threat to the system but they are seen as radicals and eccentrics who have nothing to offer their students. They interrupt the university curriculum and expose the anxiety of thinking, they do not teach all students but rather 'not-all students': since the 'not-all' is not any One student but neither is it the collection of students taken-together. The 'not-all' student opens up to the pre-existing trauma and operates upon it through the processes of scholarly invention. Not all students will be prepared to learn in this way. This is why the path for invention is only open to some, and it is why there is a tragedy to invention – or, as Joker would put it: 'I used to see only tragedy, now I see it's a fucking comedy!'

I return nonetheless to my original thread: whereas the first pair of oppositions for love involve a dialectic of 'foreclosure' and 'certainty,' the second seem to involve radical 'boundarylessness' and pragmatic 'boundary negotiation.' Put differently, the first dialectic operates upon the symbolic axis (foreclosure of the symbolic name-of-the-father, or certainty of a name-of-the-father in the real) and the second operates upon the imaginary (without imaginary ego/body or with tenuous imaginary ego/body). The first is a symbolic anchor and the second is a development and extension of that anchoring point toward a cohesive and consistent body of knowledge. Thus, from the first, S1, to the second, S2, we have the following couple: S1—>S2. It is a couple formed to rectify the subject's destitution, $. The way to formalize this is with the following vectorization: $—>S1—>S2—>a. This vectorization follows perfectly the capitalist discourse:

The couple S1-S2 offers a solution to the preceding and primordial trauma of subjective destitution by giving rise to the subject's desire (whereby desire is always the desire to go on desiring). But what precisely is this couple that is formed among S1 and S2? Jacques-Alain Miller cleverly demonstrated that it was the movement from the self-analysis of Freud (S1) toward the establishment of transference among the analytic couple (S2): 'Lacan teaches us [that] the structure of analytic experience derives from this couple of signifiers, S1 and S2, and where the problem is of the logical link between them' (Miller, 1988). However, this coupling always conceals a third: $, which is the trauma that gives rise to the coupling itself:

> Lacan's paired signifiers S1 and S2, a couple which conceals the third it nevertheless includes, namely the interval which separates them. [Freud writes that] 'the subject strips the trauma of its affective cathexis; so that what remains in consciousness is nothing but its ideational content, which is perfectly colorless and is judged to be unimportant.' (Miller, [2019])

When one couples – Miller claims that 'psychoanalysis is now practiced in couples' – one establishes or invents an Other as the receptacle for knowledge; through the analyst the analysand enjoys his unconscious and makes himself believe that decipherable knowledge is there hidden within his psyche. This is fundamentally different from recognizing that the S1 is all-alone, unlinked from the symbolic Other, as the basis for a certain delusion.

We can discern in both certainty and boundary negotiation modes of tranquilizing the overwhelming jouissance which threaten a communicative system. But we should not conclude that there is a true dialectic among our oppositions. Indeed, for psychotic systems, there is no possible higher arrangement, there is no Hegelian 'Aufhebung.' Dialectics should imply a movement through the symbolic by way of the linguistic operation known as metaphor. This movement is supposed to open up a space outside of primordial alienation – it is supposed to separate the subject from an overwhelming jouissance. The elementary particles of speech and language ('signifiers') could have relieved the subject of his environmental alienation by absorbing some of the jouissance (thereby allowing it to disappear). Lacan claimed that 'the signifier of this Aufhebung […] inaugurates by disappearance' (Lacan, 1977: 288). Although Lacanian clinical technique once operated according to dialectical substitutions (see Lacan, 1966: 216), today, increasingly, the dialectic has stalled, and another possibility presents itself. The linguistic operation of metonymy gets the upper-hand over metaphor. We can witness this in the prevalence of 'memes' and 'emojis' used for everyday textual communication, demonstrating that sign languages prevail over symbolic languages. What are 'sign languages?' These are self-referential languages of the body. They refer only to themselves, independent of any shared symbolic apparatus.

Whereas metaphor separates the real through substitution – the desire of the Other is effaced to some extent by the introduction of a primary signifier – metonymy broadens the scope of the originating condition by crystallizing jouissance into a 'sign.' In both cases, the aim is to achieve some distance from the overwhelming trauma of jouissance. In this sense, a 'sign' is a form of jouissance management that does not partake in the logic of the signifier. When there has been a foreclosure of the symbolic signifier, the subject's only recourse is to engage in the continuous process of metonymic invention from the void itself. What stands out most about Niklas Luhmann's communicative theory of love is the fact of the system's radical instability. Unbeknownst to Luhmann, this is a consequence of the inability for any particular system to separate adequately from the threatening environment. Hence, from the perspective of a system there is either (1) no outer communicative reality, since it is all non-sensical vis-à-vis the code and its own autonomous system of meaning, or else (2) there is too much communicative reality (e.g., the overwhelming noise of the environment in relation to the 'signal' of the code). In both cases, there is a problem of 'signal' and 'noise.' In such a circumstance, there must be the invention of jouissance management which would reduce noise into sign or signal.

There is often a refusal to accept and work through the traumatic void. Yet, it is the void which provides the basis for any phallic communicative code. It is this relationship of code to void that is responsible for the fragile instability of any system. The Lacanian word for this void at the heart of any phallic code is sinthome. From the perspective of the code and its body of communication, sinthome cannot be interpreted in any meaningful way. The sinthome simultaneously organizes a defence against environment noise and internal systemic destruction. The love letter is therefore a nonsensical process of writing addressed to nobody, it is the development of a body of meaning around the sinthomatic expression 'I love you.' The sinthome is what ultimately anchors the phallic code after the collapse of the Name/No-of-the-Father, and it is what produces the fiction of a love which nonetheless determines the subject toward the established of a lost or missing sexual relationship. Though a communicative system may have already constructed a mode of self-referential stabilization, it may nonetheless remain volatile, endlessly threatened by the twin problems of environmental pressure and self-defacement.

Although systems typically assert techniques of narcissistic boundary defence and code extension, a better and more enduring solution – indeed, it is the only intersubjective solution – involves reconstituting the system around the traumatic void and constructing a know-how regarding its void-function. The void is the inherent impetus for code generation, but it is also the basis for the establishment of discursive certainty. The autonomy of a system can therefore be maintained through an identification with an underlying nonsensical traumatic void, and this is the basis of a sharable truth: the only rapport, the only relationship possible, between two systems, is one communicated on the basis of trauma; though the experience of trauma is isolated and singular, there is, in the very form of trauma, a shared experience of suffering. I propose the French word 'autonomie' for this possibility of intersubjective coupling because it offers a homophonic counterpoint to the Lacanian Name/No-of-the-Father. 'Auto' implies 'self' and 'non' or 'nom' points toward the nomination of a code of prohibition which facilitates boundary construction and negotiation. In the absence of an anchored Name/No-of-the-father, the system involves itself in the autonomous construction of its grammar/law. Does this not explain why it was that Lacan claimed in his seminar on James Joyce and the sinthome that 'one can make do without the Name-of-the-Father, provided it is put to use' (Lacan, 2016). The Name-of-the-Father is used by the autonomous system rather than anchored to it as a transcendental guarantee.

2. Indian Capitalism

What is the difference between using a Name-of-the-Father and having one anchor a system as a transcendental guarantee? Consider the following example. While working in Pune, India, I realized that the system of traffic was quite different from what I was used to in America. Whereas America has traffic signs and lights, and an entire assortment of traffic laws and norms, India, it seems, is known for its chaotic traffic. To the outsider, this may seem like chaos (whereby the most assertive driver ultimately makes it to his destination while the selfless driver remains stuck forever) in reality there is a constant negotiation of those who are driving in the crowd. Whereas America has some sort of transcendental symbolic guarantee in the form of street lights, stop signs, and so on (at least to some relative extent), India has an assortment of individuals who are constantly in the process of boundary negotiation (the laws are produced on whim, organically, and immanently). Similarly, I have witnessed on multiple occasions the ongoings of Indian families in relation to young developing children; although I cannot generalize, I nonetheless think it is noteworthy. What I have witnessed is that the infant interacts freely, without any transcendental symbolic boundaries (e.g., children are not penned into a zone of the home, there are no enduring rules that are formed as absolutes by parental authorities, etc.) such that the paternal function is to provide affection while pragmatically introducing laws – fleeting laws – which must be repeated endlessly. And so the laws are not installed, they are endlessly reintroduced. For example, a child who wishes to play with a pair of sunglasses will reach for them, and the parent will say 'no' but leave the glasses in place. The child will move onto a different object. And then return at a later time to the sunglasses.

It is the same among Indian drivers in traffic. Within India, there are no discernible external traffic laws, but there are, nonetheless, quick decisions made by each driver as they push their way through traffic. Once I watched as an elderly Indian man attempted to negotiate his way through traffic on foot. He found a large stick and pushed it across the road, holding it in his hand. Having now stopped all of the traffic in one quick movement, he proceeded to walk across the busy intersection. Did that stick not function for him as an invention, that is, as a Name-of-the-Father when the transcendental and external one was missing? Without traffic laws, Indians constantly invent solutions such as this one. Indeed, I have not ceased to be amazed by the level of ingenuity within Indian culture. For example, rickshaw drivers use rubber bands to secure their cell phones (their GPS) onto their steering wheels, etc. This inventiveness has become a bit of a joke among Indians themselves and they invented a word to describe it: 'jugaad.' Jugaad is a Hindi colloquial term which translates roughly into 'hack.' One 'hacks' one's way around in Indian society. This term has become so important in recent scholarly commentary because of Jaideep Prabhu who argued that Indians will need jugaad as an 'important way out of the current economic crisis in developed [and emerging] economies' (as quoted in Sonwalker, 2013). The function of inventing a name-of-the-father is such that it secures for the Indian some space from the overwhelming and volatile boundary negotiations that occur regularly within the real of his or her experience. Meditation, in this case, is also a stick, in that it provides some space or distance from the proximity of the Other within the real. If the reader can withstand another minor detour, I would like to explain how this relates to American capitalism. What follows is a reproduction of a diary entry I wrote during my first few weeks in India during the summer of 2018.

> For only a few moments I could see the sun fighting its way through the rain clouds to provide me with a couple of purple rays. They shot from beyond the mountain, reminding me of the greenery that gives hope to the otherwise brown blowing sands of India. I stood at my balcony, recognizing that I am amidst one of the most beautiful sceneries on earth. Yet, in the distance I can see crowds of dogs fighting with one another. Their yelps echo into the distance, layered upon other dog yelps from another corner of the city. I turn away from the green and gaze down and left. There I am reminded that beautiful India is overrun by shops. Each shop consists of nothing but this or that. You would be confused if you were actually looking for something. Last week, I went to a 'key smith' whose shop consisted of a sign: 'Premium Service.' Upon entering his shop, I stared at an empty and unfinished building, littered with garbage, and, in the corner, there were two dogs fucking. At the center of it all, there was an old machine sitting upon some rocks. It was from this machine that he cut a key for me, charging me an unusual sum of 500 rupees. The key didn't work.

That is how it goes: to Americans in India, the belief is that they are being scammed. They cannot understand that India is a culture of endless negotiation. Twice this week, I was returned the wrong change. Prices are increased because of the color of my skin. They sell me products that I do not need, and they grossly inflate their overall quality and function: everything is a 'premium service' and everything is always of the 'highest quality.' A woman from Mumbai informed me that 'in India, everything is packaging, it doesn't matter what is actually inside of the package.' The problem is therefore not that India has not yet entered into the latest stage of capitalism, although this was what Pune's spiritual leader, Osho, claimed in response to Gandhi's socialism. Rather, its culture – mostly Hindu, athough, admittedly, there are many other religions as well – is thoroughly saturated in capitalist ideology (by capitalist, I mean in terms of the Lacanian capitalist discourse). You choose your God: in Pune, it is Ganesha, but, in another area of India, it is his father, Shiva. Twice last week I was approached by strange women who requested that I join them in a threesome with their boyfriends. I read online that more than 70% of Indian women cheat on their husbands, and around 50% of the men have accepted it as a part of their 'lifestyle.'

As I wander the street near my university, I meet a middle aged woman playing a frightening but alluring drum, and beside her was her child. The child, approximately 6 year sold, is not wearing a shirt, but has what appears to be a traditional dress around his waist. Leaning upon his shoulder is a braided whip. He asks me for money, and I reply: 'Nahin.' He insists, turning around to show me his back: it is covered in scars and cuts from his whip. His scam is as follows: if you refuse to give him some money, he will whip himself while his mother watches.

This is capitalist culture. Why do some of their gods have elephant heads, and so on? I asked, and there was no satisfying answer. I had to research the question. Ganesha was beheaded by his father Shiva. He holds in his hand also a broken tusk. When the symbolic has not taken hold, it returns within the real: animals with broken tusks instead of humans with castration anxiety. The overwhelming intensity of the social bond leads one to meditation. No wonder Osho — the celebrated figure of Pune — who so often enjoyed the festivals and sexuality of the body was nonetheless forced to introduce meditative practices.

Duane Rousselle

Indeed, the festival culture of India, the endless celebrations, are no different to me than those of Ellen Degeneres whose pain is to celebrate and dance for every episode. A model from Pune informed me that she never likes to leave her home. The festivals and dancing are too overwhelming for her. She much prefers to hide away in her apartment. This is meditation too. In every case, the triumph comes from distance from the intensity of the imperative to enjoy oneself, to celebrate, and to therefore suffer. Promiscuity is as high as I've ever seen it here. Osho's critique of Gandhi was that his socialism or anarchism would only socialize poverty. To obtain communism one requires first that India achieve capitalism. This, I suppose, makes Osho appear as a capitalist. But he is no more a capitalist than Marx, since Marx made the same point. It was Max Weber who introduced a different point of view. There is something about a culture, a spirit, which also gives rise to capitalist political economies. We should say the same about communism. The problem is not that India is not capitalist enough, but rather that India is too capitalist: it is more capitalist than America, if, broadly speaking, by capitalism we mean not 'wealth' but rather a precise structure of the social bond. Whereas America, France, and other 'Western' nations have found some sort of a solution to the problems of the intensity of capitalism by promoting secularism, it is not clear that India is going to move in that direction. It seems to me that India favours a solution similar to that of Islam: not secularism – as a hole in politics, as a place of distance between religion and economy – but rather Hinduism, as the organization of a diverse system of particularistic certainties. Indeed, Hindutva ideology has become increasingly popular in recent years, especially because of the election of Prime Minister Narendra Damodardas Modi in 2014.

Whereas capitalist discourse keeps moving, faster and faster, until it burns itself out, Indian capitalism moves even faster. In fact, I am tempted to claim that no cultural system is capable of moving faster than the Indian system. There appears to be a constant commotion. Rickshaws, and cyclists co-mingle in the streets, and move in any direction – shooting left, right, and every other direction beyond imagination. Traffic moves like so many signifiers swarming within the real. There are no external traffic laws — or those few that do exist are not at all abided

110

by, and one Indian man informed me that they are understood as 'suggestions' — and this means that all drivers execute decisions quickly. In fact, decisions are made so quickly, and changed so abruptly, that to most non-Indians it would appear as pure chaos. But this is the constant organic negotiation of one's social environment. Everyday life is a struggle for Jugaad, for invention, and, more generally, it is about hacking around.

The way out of this commotion is to invent for oneself a stick. What does this demonstrate? Psychoanalytically, we would say that there is a loss of the name-of-the-father, or, rather, an entire foreclosure of the name-of-the-father. I have seen this also in the endless ostensibly bureaucratic debates in India about what the 'naming' of a project. For example, at the university in which I currently work, a university in Pune, India, several projects have focused on the appropriate name of the project, never finding a solution. In the end, this is the one decision that can never seem to be made. Projects remain nameless for long periods of time. Yet, on the other hand, there are endless attempts to make a name for oneself. Indeed, the university at which I work is named after the individual who opened it. It is not therefore that Indians respect authority or the name-of-the-father when they go around calling their 'superiors' sir. It is rather that by calling another 'Sir' or 'Ji' a space is opened up for their own meaningful participation and engagement in a project. It is as if the endless attempt to name another 'sir' or 'ji,' or the attempt to discover a person's 'good name,' is rather a circuitous manner of pragmatically inventing a father function on whim. It is important to have and to choose the appropriate people to name 'sir' or 'Ma'am,' because this also, as a consequence, produces an understanding of who you are in relation to that person. If one person is 'sir' then you are, in effect, his inferior. And this produces some distance. It too functions as if it were a stick pressed out into traffic.

What, then, is the stick? The stick is the invention of a name-of-the-father when one appears to be lacking. It is also by consequence the invention of a space for the subject, it is the invention of desire itself. Similarly, meditation is an invention, a crucial one, used for the purposes of obtaining some distance from the crowd of signifiers that organically pervade the real everyday conditions of Indian life. This is how decision-making happens here in India. Ideas collide, and it is a complete mess. Nothing makes sense. Until, finally, somebody invents a stick: an idea, to which one remains dogmatically fixed, against which no other ideas might compare. It is only when this occurs that a space of existence can be established in the board room or in the classroom. We must always be prepared to use our sticks so that we can meaningfully engage in a hopeful world of possibilities. Yet, at the same time, it is extremely important that we recognize that this stick is nothing but a prop — this is the most important part of the prop(er name). The stick demonstrates that when the proper name ceases to function the name itself can be made use of as if it were a prop.

3. The Saint: A Counterpoint to Mastery

Lacan argued that there exists only one counterpoint to discourses of mastery: the analyst's discourse. As a counterpoint to the master discourse of capitalism, analytic discourse takes on less rather than more meaning: the analyst is no longer the one who embodies the deciphered meaning of the subject's unconscious but rather the one who becomes the pure refuse (or, rather, garbage receptacle) of meaning itself. Put another way, Lacan reasoned that the goal of analysis is to become like a saint, inasmuch as the saint is not the one who endlessly gives of his possessions or kindness but the one who becomes the reject of processes of consumerism and commodification. This was Joker's position in the final portion of the latest film. Lacan's 'Saint-Homme,' which is a French homophone of 'Sinthome,' is, like the lover, increasingly rarified; it is a status reserved only for those who 'have the right stuff.' As Bruce Fink once put it: 'either one is born with the right stuff or one is not; and if one is not, no amount of analysis will ever enable one to occupy the proper analytic position' (Fink, 2004: 12). In other words, there are very few lovers because there are very few saints, and yet, Lacan concluded that '[becoming a saint is] the way out of capitalist discourse – which will not constitute progress if it happens only for some' (Lacan,

1974: 20). The problem with saints is that there are always so few of them, by definition. Saints do not therefore constitute a movement any more than Joker and his 'followers' constituted a movement. Similarly, there will never be a movement of lovers: they are radically on their own in this world which rejects them.

We therefore have some of the key attributes of a saint: the saint is aligned with the sinthome – a working forth from the void of an inventive process of knotting together the three orders of Symbolic, Imaginary, and Real – while 'acting as trash [...] [thereby] allowing the subject of the unconscious to take him as the cause of the subject's own desire' (Lacan, 1974: 15). But what type of trash is the saint? The analyst was once understood as the receptacle for the subject's unconscious desires – a place in which the symbolic letters might be discarded – but in the new analytic discourse the analyst becomes the place from which the real unconscious might be stored: the void or lack-of-being might itself be displaced onto the couple of the analyst-analysand, and the analyst can reflect back onto the analysand this non-sensical jouissance which drives the subject toward his truth. The psychoanalytic session becomes yet another – and perhaps the final! – push toward the truth. In this case, truth is coupled with an expected meaning, and therefore betrays the nonsensical jouissance which governs it. Jacques-Alain Miller puts it like this:

> Lacan tells us in Seminar XVII, Chapter IV, that [...] there is no truth without jouissance. And yet there is no last word, no 'full' truth, when it comes to jouissance. Truth is coupled with meaning, and they form a trio with fiction. But analyses stumble upon a residue of jouissance that cannot be dealt with by truth. (Miller, 2016: 9)

The subject expects the coupling of meaning for truth as a defence against jouissance, he endlessly 'runs after the truth' (Lacan, 2004: np), but the saint finds truth in becoming 'the refuse [trash] of jouissance [itself]' (Lacan, 1974: 16). The saint interrupts the endless addictive drive toward enjoyment without recourse to the coupling of meaning; rather, the saint invents a meaning for himself. The saint stops enjoying as a commandment and becomes the enjoyment which anyway compelled him.

By contrast, the function of a code for a communicative system is to conceal the traumatic void, to smother it with an attempt at coupling with the environment. The love letter is written to couple with the lover, the religious communicative system has as its modus operandi to render its environment sacred or profane, the political communicative system aims at coupling with its environment by distinguishing between power and non-power, and so on. It does so by quilting the body of its communicative system to a central phallic code or semblance. Yet, this central code is the mark of any system's distinction from another systemic body – it cannot be understood except via the circularity of its own mode of self-reference. The code's self-referentiality is known within linguistics as 'holophrasis,' and it is typical of psychotic communicative systems. Slavoj Žižek writes that 'in such cases, suffering is not organized in the manner of neurotic systems, via condensation and displacement, but through the direct petrifaction of the signifier onto the body' (Žižek, 2005: 27). Is this not what Luhmann insists most about his communicative systems? As Eva M. Knodt, in his preface to Luhmann's Social Systems (1995) put it:

> Each of these systems reproduces itself recursively on the basis of its own, system-specific operations. Each of them observes itself and its environment, but whatever they observe is marked by their unique perspective, by the selectivity of the particular distinctions they use for their observations. There is no Archimedian point from which this network could be contained in an all-embracing vision. (Knodt in Luhmann, 1995: xii)

The universality of Luhmann's vision is paradoxically the universality of a perspective from the one-all-alone: there are ones-all-alone. It is a universal experience of the subject, all alone in his mode of enjoyable suffering. It is this with which the 'movement' of Joker's identify, and it is similar, in some way, to the sort of metonymic identification one sees in the #MeToo movement.

The #MeToo movement attempts to constitute a 'we' of singularities – a chain of Me's rather than a pure 'we' –

metonymically or holophrastically, when the metaphor of the law has fallen. When the social link is absent a new mode of connection must be invented. Jamieson Webster and Kyoo Lee wrote:

> The phrasal slogan is such that #MeToo would say it all without telling it at all: what 'it' is, we think we know without knowing exactly, the details, what happened, including what could not or should not have happened. Yet, that's the point, we've always known. (Webster & Lee, 2018)

The problem is that the signifying chain is not properly secured, since the metonymic 'quilting points' of the discourse are discovered outside in the power of other testimonies. Each 'me' testimony secures, retroactively, the truth of the preceding through imitation. What is at stake in the movement is therefore an appeal to justice based not upon the transcendental symbolic law but rather upon the invention of a new collective morality. Slavoj Žižek has referred to this as a novel form of 'extra-legality' or populist morality, which produces the following result: the accused can only manage by avoiding appeals to the transcendental system of justice and motioning toward a feminization of masculinity.

This, in of itself, is not necessarily a 'bad' thing. The problem is rather that the new social bond offers a concerning new vision. Žižek writes that '[for #MeToo] the limits of freedom are set so narrow that even a modest debate about different grades of abuse is considered unacceptable.' The new mode of invention offers certainty without adequately dealing with the void beyond the rubric of power whereby the key question is as follows: is 'victimization a source of power' or is 'sex itself an oppressive form of power.' The code's holophrastic function can possibly retroactively determine guilt: 'you are guilty because you are guilty.' Thus, there are a number of difficult questions that will have to be pursued such as: (1) the question of victimization (as agent of a discourse) as a new mode of power, (2) the eradication of the power through bourgeois aesthetics, and (3) the problem of foreclosing the Other through fear.

For example, today's new modes of power in America operate by declaring oneself a victim publicly. Any debate that might occur is about the right to declare oneself a victim. This is a new way of constituting the 'beautiful soul syndrome,' described wonderfully by Timothy Morton:

> You, having exited this world, are good. Over there is the evil object [person], which you shun or seek to eliminate. Over here is the good subject, who feels good precisely insofar as she or he has separated from the evil world. I am now describing Hegel's beautiful soul, who claims precisely to have exited the evil world. (Morton, 2009)

The beautiful soul positions him or herself outside of the evil world in order to open him or herself up to a private luxurious space of goodness. We are now in the world of the pluralization of beautiful souls – the ones all alone. Jacques-Alain Miller puts the new situation in the following way:

> Socio-cultural stereotypes of womanliness and virility are in the process of radical transformation. Men are being invited to open up to their emotions, to love and feminise themselves; women on the contrary are undergoing a certain 'push to masculinisation': in the name of legal equality they're being driven to keep saying 'me too.' At the same time, homosexuals are claiming the same rights and symbols as heteros, like marriage and filiation. Hence a major instability in the roles, a widespread fluidity in the theatre of love, that contrasts with the fixity of yesteryear. Love is becoming 'liquid', as noted by the sociologist Zygmunt Bauman. Everyone is being led to invent their own 'lifestyle', to assume their mode of jouissance and mode of loving. Traditional scenarios are slowly becoming obsolete. Social pressure to conform hasn't disappeared, but it's on the wane. (Miller, 2013)

The only point of disagreement I have here is that 'social pressure to conform hasn't disappeared, but it's on the wane.' Žižek has claimed that social pressure is actually all the more intense. The new modes of invention force an adaptation to a new reality, one which fundamentally challenges the preceding paradigm of the law but in doing so only introduces further problems: today there will be a growing class of individuals whose reality is considered 'less real' and whose 'victimization' will be ignored, and they will have no recourse to a mode of argumentation. It becomes a war of whose reality is to be considered more real, a veritable battle of delusions.

There is a new aversion to the primordial wound of sex and sexuality. For today's capitalist discourse, Lacan claimed, we 'do away with matters of sex.' Indeed, sex is no longer a topic for conversation within #MeToo unless of course it is viewed through the prism of power and domination. Slavoj Žižek explains:

> Oscar Wilde said: 'everything in life is about sex except for sex itself. Sex is about power.' And that is what you see so clearly in #MeToo. They talk about sex all the time, but it is not really sex. For them sex is only viewed through the prism of power. It is an instrument of power, and power at its worst. Why? Because even if they have the right to complain against male domination and exploitation, their complaint is not aimed at really helping people it is aimed at using your victimization as a resource of your own power. They want power.

He argues that victimization is a new way to acquire power:

> One of the ways to acquire power in the United States is to present yourself as a victim. If you are a victim you are beyond reproach and whatever arguments you give against the person who claims to be a victim,' you are in advance accused of brutalizing the victim. #MeToo got too wrapped up in American academic life and journalist circles (intellectual circles) where it is all about power and career. To complain, to present yourself as a victim is a way to reassert your power. A new approach is required here.

Isn't it the case that we run the danger of redoubling victimization? In the new economy of jouissance, there will be those who have been victimized once through accusation and then twice through the stripping away of their right to even declare themselves a victim. We will therefore approach a key moment of resistance in the #MeToo discourse when an accused man declares himself a victim. It is as if the accuser knows at some level that to declare a man a victim is to give him more power. Žižek writes:

> I even suspect that politically correct people don't really want to resolve the problem because if the problem disappears they would have to change radically. Their whole identity is based on proclaiming yourself a victim and blaming others. If you take this away from them, they are nobody. Psychoanalysis teaches that when somebody complains you should try to identify what type of additional satisfaction or pleasure the complaining brings out for them.

Today's political battle therefore seems to be over the right to declare oneself a victim rather than the right to directly oppress or victimize. Yet, there is an additional problem of the aesthetics of the working class. Pierre Bourdieu has documented very well in his wildly popular book Distinction: A Social Critique of the Judgment of Taste that the working class – those low in social, cultural, economic, and symbolic capital – are among the most 'politically incorrect' in their everyday discourse. This apparent vulgarity is perhaps even a way that the working-class bonds with one another in America, and it explains why the working-class are today often captured by the discourse of American president Donald Trump. In erasing all vulgarities, in accelerating a culture of hyper-consent, #MeToo therefore ignores the poor and appeals to the upper and middle classes of white feminism. Žižek claims that this is a crucial point: '#MeToo was a mass movement of women, first black women, to protest their daily existence. When #MeToo exploded, it was immediately appropriated by the upper and middle-classes. And all of this class dimension — exploited blacks, working class women, etc. — disappeared.' If anything can be salvaged from #MeToo it will have to be a renewed commitment to attacking the culture of political correctness and introducing the domain of vulgarity into the social link.

Finally, #MeToo demonstrates a fundamental intolerance of the neighbour. For them, the Other must always be kept at a distance, always rejected. Žižek writes:

There is something very violent [for #MeToo] in over-proximity. The implicit view of men in political correctness is like what Sartre said: 'hell is other people.' The implicit rule is to keep the other at a distance. Whatever you do you — you smoke, you flirt, whatever — it is experienced as an aggression. The whole logic of it, of excessive #MeToo ... is very narcissistic individualistic. 'I want my peace, let the other remain at a distance.'

We can see here a foreclosure of the Other, and a compensation technique through the establishment of a metonymic chain. At some point, this chain will be threatened and the worst will occur. This is perhaps the greatest problem for #MeToo. In the foreclosure of the Other, in the endless rejection of the Other's proximity — in the rejection of love itself! — the subject will be unable to constitute an enduring social bond.

All of this is what leads me to a sort of axiom: #MeToo has given up love for a dangerous form of social bond based on radical isolation from the Other. A better strategy would be to locate within love the possibility of an encounter with the Other's lack as a mode of empathy. This, however, is the furthest of possibilities. Love is becoming all the more impossible. And, it seems to me, that the reinvention of what it means to love one another is our only revolutionary political hope. Love is the name for a social bond based upon an acceptance of the Other's lack, of the inexistence of the Other — but not of the foreclosure of the Other.

I now return to my thread concerning holophrasis and communicative systems. Žižek continues by relating the holophrastic code to the boundary or 'no saying' function of any communicative system: 'in Lacan's early accounts of holophrasis in the 1950's, he argues that it materializes the 'limit' between language and the body, 'the ambiguous intermediary zone between the symbolic and the imaginary' (Žižek, 2005: 27). If the symbolic code is built upon a hole, and if the body of a system – that which constitutes the self-referential circulation of its communicative network - is entirely dependent upon that

119

code, then metonymic holophrasis is the work of producing boundaries vis-à-vis the environment. However, what is seldom acknowledge, is that the traumatic void is also what gives birth to holophrastic processes; indeed, trauma is a push from the beyond into the refuse of the body. If it seems to us that trauma is symptomatic, then, the holophrastic communicative code might be thought of as the system's formal envelope. Jacques-Alain Miller picked up on this Lacanian expression ('formal envelope') in the following passage:

> [T]he term formal envelope poses the question of the enveloped – the symptom is not all signifier, and what this formal envelope of the symptom evokes as negative is what it envelopes of jouissance [...] Therefore, the emptying of the formal envelope of the symptom is the condition of creation, insofar as it proceeds from ex nihilo, as Lacan used to say, from nothingness (Miller, 2011).

We might locate within this passage a movement from the traditional Freudian model of the interpretable 'symbolic unconscious' toward the later Lacanian orientation of the 'real (indecipherable) unconscious.' In other words, the transition moves from a deciphering of latent interpretations of a symptom, whereby the symptom is reducible to 'all signifiers,' toward, finally, an acceptance of the fact that within a symptom there exists a kernel of non-sensical enjoyment which overflows and threatens to destroy all of subjective life. Consequently, when the non-sensical kernel of enjoyment is met without distance, without mediation, a wound in the subject's innermost sense of self occurs, a process Miller has referred to as 'subjective externality.'

The question becomes: how might this traumatic void be communicated? Perhaps we should risk the possibility that it might be communicated not with 'all signifiers' but rather through some sort of aesthetic organization. The formal envelope of the code is precisely grounded today by artistic practices. Love is a name we can give to this process of mutual recognition and communication of the trauma void. Veronica Voruz writes:

Love [as] an inscription of contingency that comes to replace castration […] in order to make do with the impossibility of the sexual relation. This form of love, arising from an acceptance of the sexual non-relation, is of the order of invention, of a savoir faire that enables one to make do with the impossibility of the Real without being the slave of the unconscious. (Voruz, 2002: 135)

Voruz's thesis is perfectly the thesis that I have been trying to pursue in this book. Here, we can see a redefinition of love via the 'late' Lacan: love is a process of invention rather than metaphorical substitution. To love has become a delicate artistic practice, a refuge from trauma. Voruz is here claiming that one is able to construct a 'know-how' or savoir-faire which releases the subject from being a slave of the real unconscious. In this case, the subject no longer feels threatened by a noisy environment but develops a sense of suffering with which he can live; it is a sense of suffering in love which is not optimal but without which the situation could be much worse: '… or worse,' indicates a foreclosure of the symbolic and a retreat into the traumatic real. It seems to me that this bleak '… or worse' possibility is what the subject gets if he forecloses the suffering vis-à-vis the name/no-of-the-father (Lacan, 2018).

4. Love Letters from Sociologists

Based on all of this, it seems to me that a love letter is best understood as a Luhmannian communicative system. A love letter erects a wall between the subject and his environment, thereby emptying that environment of any of its defining features: it is an internal environment, an environment devoid of environmental elements. The love letter is the site for the construction of an intimate environment which is internal to the letter itself. Lacan famously closed his seminar on Edgar Allan Poe's 'The Purloined Letter' with the following two enigmatic statements:

The sender, we tell you, receives from the receiver his own message in reverse form. Thus, it is that what the 'purloined letter,' nay, the 'letter in sufferance,' means is that a letter always arrives at its destination. (Lacan, 2019)

The sender of a love letter always receives what he writes back to himself without thereby breaking with the self-referentiality of his letter. This is one possible interpretation for Lacan's claim that a letter always arrives at its destination: its destination is determined afterward, after the letter has already been written, and this produces the retroactive effect of producing the determinations which pushed the lover to set pen to paper. To receive the message back in an inverted form does not imply that the letter actually reaches the loved one in her alterity, it means, rather, that the letter reaches before/ beyond the loved one. The letter reaches the subject's own phantasmatic environment. Put simply, every love letter reaches its destination because the destination is the lover himself.

But what part of the lover does the letter reach? The answer is that the lover reaches and plays with the alterity of himself, that is, the letter is the sandbox within which he enjoys his own unconscious. Colette Soler wrote that:

Love letters are paradoxical [...] because they seem to speak about the big Other [environment] [...]; but, in fact, they are made with the unconscious of the subject. Thus, they are symptoms which lie to the partner, because for the subject who writes they are only a way of enjoying his or her own unconscious. You see the paradox: the love letters are in fact a wall between subject and partner. So, we can conclude that the lover who writes too many love letters is just a lover of himself as unconscious. (Soler, 2003: 101)

We might claim that the love letter consists of a dual function: first, it upholds and extends the narcissism of the system by way of the pursuit of extensions and/or defences of a system's codified boundaries, and; second, it produces, through the writing of the letter, a beautiful sign of the system's inherent trauma. Enjoyment of the subject's own codes tranquilizes disturbances in the environment. The love letter is therefore also a mode of stabilization for the subject. Yet it is not clear sometimes whether there is a 'love letter' or the 'love of a letter.' Indeed, there may be a fundamental ambivalence of the system in that the love letter also demonstrates a certain love for the letter. These two simultaneous functions of the subject vis-à-vis environment indicate that the 'love letter' is a mode of profound subjective suffering but also a pathway toward jouissance management. The source of the subject's overwhelming enjoyment is the senseless repository of jouissance inherent in the void, but this is also what compels the subject to work toward new modes of jouissance management. Environmental noise consists of nonsensical stray signifiers (uncoupled from any signified, from any meaning) rendered consistent by the invention of a code. Consistency within Luhmannian systems are always anchored by a code. Yet, what is most interesting for now is the fact that the internal consistency of a love letter is maintained by a subject who exists in radical isolation from his environment: it is written by the subject all alone. We could rephrase this in the following way: the code-all-alone is akin in form to the 'one-all-alone' discussed by Jacques Lacan and members of the World Association of Psychoanalysis. Eric Laurent writes that:

> The 'dismantling of the defence' is not only a dismantling of the idol invested in the stead of phallic lack, but also of the circuit of the object a so as to encounter the edge of enjoyment that these circuits delimit. The consistencies are knotted around this edge. [...] Lacan proposes here an other version of the unconscious that is not composed of the effects of the signifier on an imaginary body, but one that includes the real that is the pure repetition of the same. This is what, in his last Class, Jacques-Alain Miller isolated as the dimension of the One-all-alone that repeats. There, is truly the zone outside of meaning, and outside of any guarantee. (Laurent, 2014)

The fascinating claim therefore is no longer that love is a difficulty or a doubt of suffering within the psychoanalytic clinic but rather that love is now one manner of producing a social link for the one-all-alone; put another way, love is a way of producing a link to the unconscious, to the environment, and, moreover, it is one way of opening up a subject so that the subject may simply begin to dream again. To dismantle the defensive code which isolates the subject as one-all-alone is to open up a space for investigating the real unconscious, and this is what makes a social link possible in the era of the ones-all-alone. This is why the practice of writing love letters – of falling in love with the letter – is increasingly important for the subject.

It was Jacques-Alain Miller who identified this new modality of love as a social link in the era of the ones-all-alone. On this, I shall quote him at length and then attempt an interpretation in light of the love letter:

> [L]ove is what can mediate between the ones-all-alone. Thus, saying that it is imaginary, in fact creates a difficulty. It is to say that the unconscious does not exist. The primary unconscious does not exist as knowledge. For it to become knowledge, to make it exist as knowledge, there must be love. And that is why Lacan could say at the end of his Seminar The Names of the Father: a psychoanalysis, it demands that you love your unconscious. It is the only means of establishing a relation between S1 and S2. Because in the primary state, there are only disjoint 'ones,' there are only scattered 'ones.' Therefore, a psychoanalysis demands that you love your unconscious in order to make something exist, not the sexual rapport, but the symbolic relation. (Miller, 2004)

First, we see from Miller an affirmative statement concerning love: it is not an attempt to overcome lack, but rather an attempt to mediate through the installation of lack, and to therefore construct an inadequate social link. The love of the letter is an attachment to the real unconscious since to write the love letter is to affirm that the unconscious does indeed exist. Whereas Miller once claimed that 'psychoanalysis is now practiced in couples,' what he meant is that the one-all-alone, the S1, must be made linked to the body of unconscious knowledge. This is just another way of stating that the lover must generate for himself a knowledge of his love (S2, the body of knowledge constructed by way of the circulation of his code) via the mediation of the letter. In the era of the ones-all-alone, the love letter functions not to overcome the lack of a sexual relation but precisely to introduce a symbolic cut – a challenge which would make the lover believe that the sexual relation does not exist.

In this way, the lover of the letter involves himself in the practices of courtly love. In courtly love the lover over-values his loved one and yet discovers an impossibility to their union. The union of the lovers ensures only the destruction of the subject, or rather, the trauma of their proximity. The lover remains in fidelity to the possibility of their union precisely by accepting the distance which separates them. It is even a question of whether lover's inaccessibility is constitutive of his certainty in love. Lacan makes the following claim: '[t]he feminine object is introduced [...] through the door of privation or of inaccessibility. Whatever the social position of him who functions in the role, the inaccessibility of the object is posited as a point of departure' (Lacan, 1992 [1986]: 149). The logic of sublimation – whereby an object substitutes for the lack – therefore takes on a peculiar character: the formal envelope of the loved one taken as object is revealed as a lack in of itself. Within courtly love, the loved one is not idealized in the sense of being imaginary but rather symbolized in the sense of marking out a space of distance from the jouissance of the real unconscious. This is another way to read Lacan's statement that in sublimation the object is 'elevated to the dignity of the Thing' (Lacan, 1992 [1986]: 112).

Courtly love today is not simply, as Lacan claimed, 'a refined way of making up for the absence of sexual relation by pretending that it is us who put an obstacle to it' (Lacan, 1992 [1986]: 114). It is not that courtly love is the subject's strategy of demonstrating to himself that he has a sexual relationship precisely by losing that sexual relationship. Unlike Orpheus, who perhaps had to lose in order to demonstrate to himself that he actually had something to lose in the first place, courtly love affirms rather that lack is an essential and insufferable symbolic ingredient for there being a social link. The subject produces the lack in the form of his suffering so that he can finally believe that there is no rapport between himself and his loved one. Whereas the former is a neurotic strategy for 'making up for the lack of a sexual relationship,' the latter is an autonomous strategy of self-generation vis-à-vis the whirlwind of his environment. Slavoj Žižek seems to have already begun to introduce this innovative rereading of Lacan's extensive seventh seminar on courtly love. He writes that '[t]he place of the Lady-Thing is originally empty' (Žižek, 2006: 94), which implies that she fulfills not an imaginary hole but a symbolic hole making up for the loss of the Name/No-of-the-Father.

The Lady-Thing therefore introduces the subject back into the orbit of his desire, separating him from that which feels to him as an endlessly cruel monster threatening to devour him. He writes: 'she functions as a kind of 'black hole' around which the subject's desire is structured. [...] The only way to reach the Object-Lady is indirectly, in a devious, meandering way – proceeding straight on ensures that we miss the target' (Žižek, 2005: 94). The woman-object of courtly love is not simply functioning to conceal an underlying trauma but is rather functioning to introduce relief from that trauma in the form of her cruelty: her intrusions and demands is that which the lover cannot handle, is the source of his perpetual complains. But this is also what opens him up, through her symbolic function, to the distance which pushes his desire. She is not only a woman which he must have or possess, she is a woman without whom he cannot live. She is merely an extension of the man's own narcissism, the satisfaction of a code which cuts him from within and allows him to couple with his unconscious (S1-S2).

The love letter is a symptom inasmuch as it is the formal envelope through which the lover invents a solution to his alienation within the environment. He does so by simultaneously dislocating himself from the Other while inventing for himself a substitute Other – the phallic woman substitutes for the traumatic desire of the environment. Writing a love letter becomes symptomatic at that point when the subject's isolation from his environment becomes so exacerbated that he loses himself to that same environment. Thus, it is not that the love letter dislocates himself from the environment in the sense that he feels dislocated from that environment, it is that the love letter introduces a dislocation through which the lover himself finds a sense of relief. At this point we might locate within the suffering of distance the love letter as a counterpoint to the trauma of environmental suffocation: the lover suddenly, through the love letter, knows his place in the world, forms for himself a sense of identity, his purpose is secured, and his desire has been installed. For the love of the letter, the lover finds a reason to live. The problem is that this symbolic pact must be endlessly re-secured, since the distance is tenuous and at any moment the chasm might be either overcome or so impossible as to provoke too much despair.

This is why the love letter must always be rewritten, again and again. Lacan's favoured expression 'encore' implies a repetition – but we might reinterpret it as a repetition of the tenuous link embodied by a social bond: 'en-coeur,' since love is never anymore written once and for all, the lover never writes only one love letter. The impossible enjoyment of love is therefore fragile. Colette Soler writes that 'we cannot imagine a lover who would pretend to write just one letter, once and for all' (Soler, 2003: 101). If the name/no-of-the-father had been installed it would have guaranteed the stability of the social link through repression. However, since it was not it must be continuously reinvented and renewed through psychotic invention: the lover is today in search of a certainty, forever foreclosing the temptation to doubt. No wonder the classical German sociologist Georg Simmel was so fascinated by the concepts of distance, secrecy, flirting, and so on. For Simmel the social bond is tenuous in that it must continually be constructed as a fact of subjective life. The movement from a dyadic social bond toward a triad social bond is made possible by the introduction of 'distance.' Indeed, the third person – a stranger to the dyadic bond – has as his sole function the introduction of distance into the volatile and intensely charged fusion of the dyadic relation (Simmel, 1950).

This function of symbolic 'hole' introduces for the subject a sense of distance from the primordial selflessness of environmental fusion. Simmel had an intuition of the importance of the symbolic function of distance when he wrote that:

'Triviality' connotes a certain measure of frequency, of the consciousness that a content of life is repeated, while the value of this content depends on its very opposite, a certain measure of rarity. [...] Individuality in the sense of uniqueness or rarity seems to play no role, and its non-existence, therefore, seems not to have the effect of triviality. But in dyadic relations, love, marriage, friendship [...] which do not result in higher units, the tone of triviality frequently becomes desperate and fatal. (Simmel, 1950: 126)

We can see the necessity of interrupting the dyadic relation by introducing the distance of a strange and eccentric paternal signifier such that individuality – a quality of being separate and unique from the higher form of life – cannot occur, and, indeed, becomes eclipsed. This is Simmel's lamentation for the death of the subject. Simmel marks the importance of symbolic distance as a way of producing consistency within the elements of a system's code; however, in his case, he speaks of 'elements of interaction': '[I] indicate how elements which increase distance and repel, in the relations of and with the stranger produce a pattern of coordination and consistent interaction' (Simmel, 1971 [1908]: 144). This was Georg Simmel's sociological genius: to have found within objective cultural forms a space for the emergence of subjective individuality. Only by exploring this logic further – as late Lacanian theory does – can we understand better the relationship of the subject to his environment.

Simmel could not have known the extent to which today's love requires the introduction of distance for the emergence of a subject to his environment. Thus, the love letter serves an ever more important function in the lives of lovers: it does not simply produce a wall between them but rather produces the possibility of a separation in the sexual relationship which today comes all too easy. Indeed, the sexual relationship is today pre-existent, such that love is now the rarest of possibilities. We can see once again the three-fold externalities characteristic of ordinary psychosis in the world of Simmel (and yet also his attempt at stabilization), particularly in the first few lines of his famous essay 'The Metropolis and Mental Life' ([1903] 1950): 'social externality' and 'subjective externality' are present in the opening sentence of the essay: 'the deepest problems of modern life derive from the claim of the individual to preserve the autonomy and individuality of his existence in the face of overwhelming social forces, of historical heritage, of external culture, and of the technique of life' ([1903] 1950: 409). 'Bodily externality,' the second of the threefold discrete signs of ordinary psychosis, is also implicated in the second sentence: 'The fight with nature which primitive man has to wage for his bodily existence attains in this modern form its latest transformation' (ibid.).

For Simmel, modern life, characterized by the metropolis, implies the triumph of 'objective life,' the Other's life, over 'subjective life,' whereby the subject is increasingly unable to conquer a place for himself in the universe. Simmel wrote:

> [T]he development of modern culture is characterized by the preponderance of what one may call the 'objective spirit' over the 'subjective spirit.' [...] [H]e can cope less and less with the overgrowth of objective culture. [...] [He] has become a mere cog in an enormous organization of things and powers which tear from his hands all progress, spirituality, and value in order to transform them from their subjective form into the form of a purely objective life (Simmel, [1903] 1950).

To my knowledge, Simmel was the first sociologist to introduce a concept of distance for understanding the structure and persistence of any social bond. This was foundational for his methodological approach to sociology, which he named 'Social geometry.' (If we are to emphasize another aspect of his work then we might also claim that he opened up the pathway toward a strictly 'formal sociology,' which emphasize various structures or forms of social interaction.) Social geometry begins with the relatively simple position that the social bond is constituted differently in dyadic and triadic bonds precisely on account of the latter's more complex arrangement. The introduction of a third element produces distance. Simmel's brilliant analysis is problematic only in the logical priority he has given to the external third: the third element comes from without, remains on the periphery of the social bond, like the traditional Lacanian father. A more interesting position would have been to examine the way in which the third is produced from within the fusion of the dyadic relationship itself – a fusion which in fact implies that there is only 'one.' When the name-of-the-father collapses one can only make do by locating the name-of-the-father within the real (e.g., the 'third').

The letter is one possible way to make-do without the name-of-the-father through the introduction of the third. One of the ways that we might interpret Lacan's enigmatic statement that 'a letter always arrives at its destination' is by claiming that a letter retroactively produces its own determinations. It is indeed through the writing of the letter, through the circulation of its codes, that the event of love is therefore produced, and not, as it were, vice versa. The environment is that which produces the subject, and yet, when the environment it produced by the subject it is as if the was the subject who was himself produced as a consequence of it. Take the following example from Slavoj Žižek:

> [This] logic is at work in the well-known accident from the Arabian Nights: the hero, lost in the desert, quite by chance enters a cave. There he finds three old wise men, awakened by his entry, who say to him: 'Finally you have arrived! We have been waiting for you for the last three hundred years' – as if, behind the contingencies of his life, there was a hidden hand of Fate which directed him towards the cave in the desert. This illusion is produced by a kind of short circuit between a place in the Symbolic network and the contingent element which occupies it. Whosoever finds himself at this place is the addressee, since the addressee is not defined by his positive qualities, but by the very contingent fact of finding himself at this place. [...] This is the reason why a letter always reaches its addressee: because he becomes its addressee when he is reached (Žižek, 2011)

Another way to put it: 'it is because you are here that you were always meant to come here.' A letter therefore always arrives at its destination because 'the sender always receives from the receiver his own message in reverse form' (Lacan, 2019). In this case, we can say that the letter of the real always returns, since, we cannot avoid the fact of the traumatic hole which constantly threatens the system with destruction (Žižek, 2011). Yet, it is through the movement of this hole via the love letter that the man all-alone produces the fact of woman. Lacan puts it like this:

> Believing in a woman is, thank God, a widespread state – which makes for company, one is no longer all alone, about which love is extremely fussy. Love rarely comes true, as each of us knows, and it only lasts for a time. For what is love other than banging one's head against a wall [...]? [...] A woman is a symptom. (Lacan, 1982: 169-70)

Whereas at one time Lacan claimed that 'woman is a symptom of man,' indicating, it seemed to many, that man should be cured of this affliction, then, in this statement we believe in the woman is itself a mode of stabilization for the one-all-alone (e.g., indicated, it seems to me, in Lacan's use of the phrase 'thank God'). A woman is the formal envelope of the symptom, since, for man, she becomes the code by which he sometimes lives.

V

Overview of Argument

This book began with a number of simple premises. I have claimed that love is not reducible to the experience of any intimate union. But it is also not reducible to the experience of disunion. Love is rather paradoxical in that it fosters a connection precisely through the sharing of isolation. Similarly, love is not reducible to understanding or empathy – and it is not the consequence of successful communication – because it is essentially narcissistic in its structure. Love is a communicative channel that is opened up at the limits of communication, when the entirety of the communicative system breaks down, as a rupture and trauma which sustains the communicative edifice. It exists as a profound possibility during those moments when there is no understanding among partners. Love is also not reducible to the fall from understanding, the giving up on the desire for possession, and so on, since this is only the attitude which characterizes the preliminary possibility of any love encounter. It must also include a moment of endurance in time, a manner of sustaining the tension of difference which defines the fact of there being at least two subjects. Therefore, I reserve the concept of love to describe the entire process of a love event: (1) acceptance of the inability to possess the other, (2) the fall into non-communication and non-understanding, (3) the movement toward a new definition of eternity from within the finite world of the senses, and, finally, (4) the acceptance of a sphere of communication that one constructs as a certainty.

Yet, at the same time, I recognize – and cannot help but accept – the fact that religious social bonds constitutes the spirit of love, so much so that love, which is ever so connected to the emergence of subjectivity, must be understood differently according to the different religious discourses. It seems to me that any attempt to define a universal 'humanism' shall conflate the discourses into one, and this seems to me to be a deceptive move of power. Indeed, this was the game that Christian-secular discourse has played very well over the last few decades, and it shall be our objective to articulate another modality of love beyond the Christian hegemony. Yet, at the same time, I am willing to admit that there are some universal aspects to love; the problem is that the universality of the experience of love trans-mutates depending upon contextually specific circumstances. Whereas the concept of lack defines a universal experience – indeed, it is so universal that Slavoj Žižek has recently argued that it can be used to understand the very structure of reality – there are nonetheless different discursive structures which respond to lack: psychotics foreclose lack such that there is a lack of lack, finding themselves entirely alienated within the real by the conflation of the symbolic; neurotics repress lack and therefore function consciously as if they were lacking nothing at all, and; perverts and ordinary psychotics occupy the tension between these two positions, on one and the other side of lack, endlessly trying to bring lack into existence.

Could we not say something similar about love? Whereas sex can tell us something important about the fundamental incompleteness of reality itself, love, as what makes up for sex, can tell us not only about itself but also about sex. Love has inscribed within its own domain of experience, as what never stops being not written, the fact of sex and sexuality. Thus, it is not that there is love on the one side and sex on the other, but rather that love is what happens to sex when there is a subjective response to his or her own sexual destiny. Thus, finally, love must include also this domain of sex, it must, in the end, also include a response to the impossibility of sexual union. This is why love includes not only the 'fall' but also an attempt to construct a zone of epistemological certainty that will endure in time. It is our task to bring love and sex back together, to find there within sexual reality the possibility to love again. Thus, to the age-old question 'is it better to have loved and to have lost than to have never have loved at all?' we should answer the following: one cannot help but love, and, moreover, one cannot help but define love precisely in terms of loss. Georges Bataille once remarked about the laws of the general economy – the excessive laws that destroy all foundations – that they function whether or not the human is aware of them; we shall say the same of love. He concluded that it is better to make our peace with this fact and use it to our advantage than to have it determine us from behind our backs. And so it is the same with love.

BIBLIOGRAPHY

Adler, Robyn. (2018) 'To Give Body to the Idea is Not Easy,' As Retrieved on July 7th 2019 from <https://www.academia.edu/37255805/To_give_body_to_the_idea_is_not_easy_Lacan_Circle_of_Australia_Conference_2018>

Aguirre, Maria Cristina. (2018) 'Report on the 'Delights of the Ego' – Clinical Study Days 11,' *Lacanian Compass.* As Retrieved on July 16th 2019 from <https://www.lacaniancompass.com/csd-archive>

Badiou, Alain. (2013) *Lacan: Anti-Philosophy 3* (Kenneth Reinhard & Susan Spitzer, Eds.). New York, NY: Columbia University Press.

Badiou, Alain. (2012) *In Praise of Love* (Peter Bush, Trans.). New York, NY: The New Press.

Badiou, Alain. (2012) *The Subject of Change* (Duane Rousselle, Ed.). New York, NY: Atropos Press.

Badiou, Alain. (2006) 'Bodies, Languages, Truths,' *Lacan.com.* As Retrieved on August 22nd, 2019 from <https://www.lacan.com/badbodies.htm>

Brown, George Spencer. (1969) *Laws of Form.* London: Allen & Unwin.

Butler, Judith. (2004) 'Bracha's Eurydice,' *Theory, Culture & Society.* Vol. 21., No. 1: pp. 95-100.

Dante, Alighieri. (1995) *Dante's Inferno* (Mark Musa, Trans., Ed.). Indiana University Press.

Davenport, William. (1966) 'Book Review: Social Structure and Personality,' *American Anthropologist.* Vol. 68: pp. 274-6.

Durkheim, Emile. (1897) *Le Suicide.* Paris: Ancienne Librairie Germer Bailliere.

Ettinger, Bracha L. (2017) 'To Feel the World's Pain and Its Beauty: Brad Evans Interviews Bracha L. Ettinger,' *London Review of Books.* As Retrieved on June 29th, 2019 from https://lareviewofbooks.org/article/feel-worlds-pain-beauty/#!

Ettinger, Bracha L. (2001) 'Wit(h)nessing Trauma and the Matrixial Gaze: From Phantasm to Trauma, from Phallic Structure to Matrixial Sphere,' *Parallax,* Vol. 7., No. 4: pp. 89-114.

Fink, Bruce. (2014) *Against Understanding: Cases and Commentary in a Lacanian Key, Volume 2.* New York, NY: Routledge.

Fink, Bruce. (2004) *Lacan to the Letter: Reading Ecrits Closely.* University of Minnesota Press.

Fink, Bruce. (1995) *The Lacanian Subject: Between Language and Jouissance.* Princeton University Press.

Freud, Sigmund. (1949) 'Inhibitions, Symptoms, and Anxiety,' *The International Psychoanalytic Library* (Alex Strachey, Trans.). Toronto, ON: The Hogarth press.

Graybill, Rhiannon. (2018) 'Caves of the Hebrew Bible: A Speleology,' *Biblical Interpretation* Vol. 26. pp. 1-22.

Gueguen, Pierre-Gilles. (2010) 'On Women and the Phallus,' *The Symptom,* Vol. 11. As Retrieved on July 3rd, 2019 from <https://

www.lacan.com/symptom11/on-women.html>

Hernes, Tor., & Tore Bakken. (2003) 'Implications of Self-Reference: Niklas Luhmann's Autopoiesis and Organization Theory,' *Organization Studies*, Vol. 24., No. 9: pp. 1511-35.

Kierkegaard, Soren. (1847) *Works of Love*. Unknown.

King, Anthony. (2004) *The Structure of Social Theory*. New York, NY: Routledge.

King, Michael., and Chris Thornhill. (2003) *Niklas Luhmann's Theory of Politics and Law*. Palgrave MacMillan.

Krause, Detlef. (2005) *Luhmann Lexicon* (4th Editiion). Lucius & Lucius, Stuttgart.

Lacan, Jacques. (2019) 'Seminar on the Purloined Letter,' *Lacan. com*. As Retrieved on July 21st 2019 from <https://www.lacan. com/purloined.htm>

Lacan, Jacques. (2018) *The Seminar of Jacques Lacan, Book XIX: … Or Worse* (Adrian Price, Trans., Jacques-Alain Miller, Ed.). Polity Books.

Lacan, Jacques. (2018b) *The Seminar of Jacques Lacan, Book IV: The Object Relation*. [Private Copy, Unpublished]

Lacan, Jacques. (2018) *The Seminar of Jacques Lacan, Book XIX: … or worse* (A. R. Price, Trans., Jacques-Alain Miller, Ed.). Polity Books.

Lacan, Jacques. (2016) *The Seminar of Jacques Lacan, Book XXIII: The Sinthome* (A. R. Price, Trans., Jacques-Alain Miller, Ed.). Polity Books.

Lacan, Jacques. (2015) *The Seminar of Jacques Lacan, Book VIII:*

Transference (Bruce Fink, Trans., Jacques-Alain Miller, Ed.).
Polity Press.

Lacan, Jacques. (2007) *The Seminar of Jacques Lacan, Book XVII: The Other Side of Psychoanalysis* (Russell Grigg, Trans., Jacques-Alain Miller, Trans.). New York, NY: W. W. Norton & Company.

Lacan, Jacques. (2004) *The Four Fundamental Concepts of Psycho-analysis* (Alan Sheridan, Trans., Jacques-Alain Miller, Trans.). Karnac Books.

Lacan, Jacques. (1999) *The Seminar of Jacques Lacan, Book XX: Encore* (Bruce Fink, Trans., Jacques-Alain Miller, Ed.). New York, NY: W. W. Norton & Company.

Lacan, Jacques. (1992) [1986] *The Seminar of Jacques Lacan, Book VII: The Ethics of Psychoanalysis* (D. Porter, Trans., Jacques-Alain Miller, Eds.). London: Routledge.

Lacan, Jacques. (1991) [1969] *Le Seminaire, Livre XVII: L'envers de la psychanalyse, 1969-1970* (Jacques-Alain Miller, Ed.). Paris: Seuil.

Lacan, Jacques. (1988) *The Seminar of Jacques Lacan, Book I: Freud's Papers on Technique, 1953-1954* (John Forrester, Trans., Jacques-Alain Miller, Ed.). Cambridge: Cambridge University Press.

Lacan, Jacques. (1982) *Feminine Sexuality* (Juliet Mitchell and Jacqueline Rose, Trans., Ed.). New York, NY: W. W. Norton & Company.

Lacan, Jacques. (1977) *The Seminar of Jacques Lacan, Book XI: The Four Fundamental Concepts of Psychoanalysis* (Jacques-Alain

Miller, Ed., Alan Sheridan, Trans.). London: Hogarth Press and

Institute of Psycho-Analysis.

Lacan, Jacques. (1977b) *Ecrits: A Selection* (Alan Sheridan, Trans., Jacques-Alain Miller, Ed.). London: Tavistock Publications.

Lacan, Jacques. (1975) 'Le Seminaire, Livre XXII, RSI: 1974-1975,' in *Ornicar?*, Nos. 2-5.

Lacan, Jacques. (1974) *Television* (Jacques-Alain Miller, Ed.). W. W. Norton & Company.

Lacan, Jacques. (1972) 'Du Discours Psychoanalytique,' in *Lacan in Italia, 1953-1978* (Contri G. B., Ed), Milan: La Salamandra: pp. 32-55.

Lacan, Jacques. (1966-1967) *Le Seminaire, 1966-1967, Livre XIV. La Logique du Fantasme.* [Unpublished Seminar]

Lacan, Jacques. (1966) *Ecrits.* Paris: Seuil.

Laruelle, Francois. (2013) *Principles of Non-Philosophy* (Nicola Rubczak & Anthony Paul Smith, Trans.) Bloomsbury Academic.

Laurent, Eric. (2014) 'On the Real in a Psychoanalysis,' Orientation Text for the IXth Congress of the World Association of Psychoanalysis. As Retrieved on July 29th 2019 from <http://www.congresamp2014.com/en/template.php?file=Textos/Du-reel-dans-une-psychanalyse_Eric-Laurent.html>

Luhmann, Niklas. (1998) [1982] *Love as Passion: The Codification of Intimacy.* Stanford, CA: Stanford University Press.

Luhmann, Niklas. (1995) *Social Systems* (John Bednarz, Trans.). Stanford, CA: Stanford University Press.

Marx, Karl. (1844) 'Human Requirements and Division of

Labour Under the Rule of Private Property,' *Economic and Philosophical Manuscripts of 1844.* As Retrieved on July 14th, 2019 from <https://www.marxists.org/archive/marx/works/1844/manuscripts/needs.htm>

Miller, Jacques-Alain. [2019] 'H2O: Suture in Obsessionality,' As Retrieved on September 3rd, 2019 from <https://www.lacan.com/suture.htm>

Miller, Jacques-Alain. (2018) 'The Divine Details,' *Lacanian Ink,* Vol. 52. New York, NY: Wooster Press. pp. 28-51.

Miller, Jacques-Alain. (2016) 'Truth is Coupled with Meaning,' *Hurly-Burly.* As Retrieved on August 21st, 2019 from <https://halshs.archives-ouvertes.fr/halshs-01720558/document>

Miller, Jacques-Alain. (2015) 'Ordinary Psychosis Revisited,' *Lacanian Ink.* Vol. 46. New York, NY: Wooster Press. pp. 138-67.

Miller, Jacques-Alain. (2013) 'On Love,' *Art & Thoughts.* Dec. 2013. As Retrieved on October 19th 2019 from <https://artandthoughts.fr/2013/12/03/jacques-alain-miller-on-love/>

Miller, Jacques-Alain. (2011) 'Reflections on the Formal Envelope of the Symptom,' *The Symptom,* Vol. 16. As Retrieved on July 17th 2019 from <https://www.lacan.com/symptom16/reflections.html>

Miller, Jacques-Alain. (2004) 'Conference of Jacques-Alain Miller in Comandatuba,' IV Congress of the World Association of Psychoanalysis in Comandatuba – Bahia, Brasil. As Retrieved on July 29th, 2019 from <http://2012.congresoamp.com/en/template.php?file=Textos/Conferencia-de-Jacques-Alain-Miller-en-Comandatuba.html>

Miller, Jacques-Alain. (2002) 'Two Intuitions in Milan,' As Retrieved on October 18th, 2019 from <https://londonsociety-

nls.org.uk/The-Laboratory-for-Lacanian-Politics/Some-Research-Resources/Miller_Milanese-Intuitions-1-2.pdf>

Miller, Jacques-Alain. (1988) 'A and *a* in Clinical Structures,' Lacan.com. As Retrieved on September 3rd 2019 from <https://www.lacan.com/symptom6_articles/miller.html>

Morton, Timothy. (2009) 'Beautiful Soul Syndrome,' Unpublished Lecture at UCLA.

Nietzsche, Friedrich. (1882) *Die Frohliche Wissenschaft*. Chemnitz.

Newman, Saul. (2001) *From Bakunin to Lacan: Anti-Authoritarianism and the Dislocation of Power*. Roman & Littlefield.

Parsons, Talcott. [1958] (2016) 'Social Structure and the Development of Personality: Freud's Contribution to the Integration of Psychology and Sociology,' *Psychiatry: Interpersonal Biological Processes*. Vol. 21, No. 4: pp. 321-40.

Pope John Paul II. (1981) *Original Unity of Man and Woman, Catechesis on the Book of Genesis*. Boston: St. Paul Editions.

Rabbi Dow Marmur. (2018) 'A Place for Atheists in Judaism,' *The Canadian Jewish News*. As Retrieved on July 8th, 2019 from <https://www.cjnews.com/perspectives/opinions/a-place-for-atheists-in-judaism>

Racki, Gabriel. (2018) 'Ordinary Palpitations,' in *Papers 7.7.7.*, No. 1., As Retrieved on June 18th 2019 from <https://congresoamp2018.com/wp-content/uploads/2017/05/PAPERS-7.7.7.-N%C2%B01-English.pdf>

Recalcati, Massimo. (2020) *In Praise of Forgiveness*. Polity Books.

Rousselle, Duane. (2019) *Jacques Lacan and American Sociology: Be*

Wary of the Image. Palgrave Macmillon.

Rousselle, Duane. (2019b) *Gender, Sexuality, and Subjectivity: A Lacanian Perspective on Identity, Language, and Queer Theory.* Routledge.

Seidman, Steven. (2014) *The Social Construction of Sexuality.* New York, NY: W. W. Norton & Company.

Seynhaeve, Bernard. (2019) 'Urgent!' (Philip Dravers, Trans.), As Retrieved on July 7th, 2019 from <http://www.amp-nls. org/page/gb/332/argument>

Simmel, Georg. (1971) [1908] 'The Stranger,' in *Georg Simmel: On Individuality and Social Forms* (Donald N. Levine, Trans, Ed.). Chicago: The University of Chicago Press. pp. 143-9.

Simmel, Georg. (1950) 'Quantitative Aspects of the Group,' in *The Sociology of Georg Simmel* (Kurt H. Wolff, Trans., Ed.). Glencoe, IL: The Free Press. pp. 87-174.

Simmel, Georg. (1950) [1903] 'The Metropolis and Mental Life,' in *The Sociology of Georg Simmel* (Kurt H. Wolff, Trans., Ed.). Glencoe, IL: The Free Press. pp. 409-24.

Stavrakakis, Yannis. (1999) *Lacan and the Political.* London: Routledge.

St. Ignatius of Loyola. (1914) *Spiritual Exercises of St. Ignatius of Loyola* (Father Elder Mullan, Trans.). New York, NY: P.J. Kenedy & Sons.

Soler, Colette. (2003) 'The Paradoxes of the Symptom in Psychoanalysis,' *The Cambridge Companion to Lacan* (Jean-Michel Rabate, Eds.). New York, NY: Cambridge University Press. pp. 86-101.

Sonwalker, Prasun. (2013) 'Cambridge Expert Says Indian 'Jugaard' is Lesson to World,' *Hindustan Times.* As Retrieved on October 18th 2019 from <https://www.hindustantimes.com/india/cambridge-expert-says-indian-jugaad-is-lesson-to-world/story-M3q6vFu8tEPj8eSNsAJo5M.html>

Tutt, Daniel. (2019) 'A Lacanian Reading of Joker,' As Retrieved on October 18th 2019 from <https://danieltutt.com/2019/10/09/a-lacanian-reading-of-joker/>

Weber, Max. (2009) [1905] *The Protestant Ethic and the Spirit of Capitalism.* Norton Critical Editions.

Weick, Karl E. (1977) 'Enactment Processes in Organizations,' in *New Directions in Organizational Behaviour* (B. Staw and G. R. Salancik, Eds.). Chicago, IL: Vlair Press. pp. 267-300.

Webster, Jamieson., Kyoo Lee. (2018) 'The Formative Power of Metony#metoo,' *Studies in Gender and Sexuality.* Vol. 19., No. 4: pp. 249-53.

Vanheule, Stijn. (2016) 'Capitalist Discourse, Subjectivity and Lacanian Psychoanalysis,' *Frontiers in Psychology.* Vol. 7. Pp. 1-14.

Vanheule, Stijn. (2011) *The Subject of Psychosis: A Lacanian Perspective.* Palgrave Macmillan.

Voruz, Veronica. (2002) 'Acephalic Litter, as a Phallic Letter,' *Re-Inventing the Symptom: Essays on the Final Lacan* (Like Thurston, Ed.). New York, NY: Other Press. pp. 111-40.

Žižek, Slavoj. (2019) *Sex and the Failed Absolute.* Bloomsbury.

Žižek, Slavoj. (2015) 'Our Fear of Falling in Love,' [Video] As Retrieved on July 7th 2019 from <https://www.youtube.com/watch?v=OabTK7y7d6E&t=8s>

Žižek, Slavoj. (2012) 'Only a Suffering God Can Save Us,' *God in Pain: Inversions of Apocalypse*. New York, NY: Seven Stories Press.

Žižek, Slavoj. (2011) 'Why Does a Letter Always Arrive at its Destination?,' *The Symptom,* Vol. 16., As Retrieved on July 17th 2019 from <https://www.lacan.com/symptom16/why.html>

Žižek, Slavoj. (2008) *The Sublime Object of Ideology*. New York, NY: Verso Books.

Žižek, Slavoj. (2006) 'Psychoanalysis and the Neighbor,' in *The Neighbor: Three Inquiries in Political Theology* (Slavoj Žižek, Eric L. Santner). Chicago: The University of Chicago Press. pp. 11-75.

Žižek, Slavoj. (2005) *The Metastases of Enjoyment: Six Essays on Women and Causality*. Verso.

Žižek, Slavoj. (2003) *The Puppet and the Dwarf: The Perverse Core of Christianity*. MIT Press.

Zupančič, Alenka. (2017) *What is Sex?* MIT Press.

Zupančič, Alenka. (2012) 'Sexual Difference and Ontology,' *e-flux journal,* Vol. 32. As Retrieved on June 29th 2019 from http://worker01.e-flux.com/pdf/article_8948423.pdf

INDEX

#MeToo, 115, 117, 118, 119
Abrahamic, 12, 13, 14, 15, 18
Abu Dharr, 34
Abu Huraira, 62
Adam and Eve, 3, 31
Agape love, 9
Alain Badiou, 25, 36, 41, 53, 79
Alenka Zupančič, 23, 31, 46
Alt-Right, 92
Arthur Rimbaud, 58
Bernard Seynhaeve, 28
Black Panther, 92
Bollywood, 56
Bracha L. Ettinger, 34, 36, 68, 82, 90
Bruce Fink, 50, 52, 112
Calvinism, 80
Charles Horton Cooley, 63
Chicago, 64
Colette Soler, 122, 127
Daniel Tutt, 92
Dante, 53, 54, 56
Edgar Allan Poe, 121
Ellen DeGeneres, 17
Emile Durkheim, 1, 64, 66, 68
Eric Laurent, 123
Francois Laurelle, 70
Freud, 5
G. K. Chesterton, 43
Georg Simmel, 9, 63, 127, 128
George Herbert Mead, 63
George Spencer Brown, 76
Georges Bataille, 50, 134
Gilles Deleuze, 84
Jacques-Alain Miller, 18, 40, 41,
49, 59
Jaideep Prabhu, 108
James Joyce, 45, 106
Jamieson Webster, 114
Jerry Seinfeld, 50
Jesuits, 39, 40, 41
Judith Butler, 36
Kant, 4
Karl Marx, 42, 52, 56, 68, 80, 86
Khadijah, 29
Kierkegaard, 12, 13
Lord Ganesha, 17
Lord Shiva, 17
Ludwig Feuerbach, 43
Maria Cristina Aguirre, 32
Marshall McLuhan, 32
Massimo Recalcati, 25
Max Stirner, 43
Max Weber, 16, 63, 65, 80, 110
Michel Foucault, 80
Moses, 16, 19, 37
Mount Sinai, 19
Narendra Damodardas Modi, 110
New Lacanian School, 28
Nietzsche, 21
Niklas Luhmann, 9, 68, 69, 70, 71
Norm Macdonald, 61
One-All-Alone, 89
Orpheus, 26, 27, 88, 125
Osho, 17, 109, 110
Passion of the Christ, 35
Pierre Bourdieu, 118
Pierre-Gilles Gueguen, 27
Plato, 29

Pope John Paul II, 3
Protestantism, 80
Quebec, 30
Rabbi Dow Marmur, 43
Rat Man, 96
Rhiannon Graybill, 38
Salifiyah, 15
Saul Newman, 51
Shia, 41
Slavoj Žižek, 23, 25, 31, 37, 39
St. Ignatius of Loyola, 28, 29, 87
Stijn Vanheule, 72, 100
T. S. Eliot, 15
Talcott Parsons, 75, 84

The Joker, 92, 93
Timothy Morton, 115
Trump, 81, 118
Upanishads, 54
Veronica Voruz, 120
Walter Benjamin, 81
Wolf Man, 96
World Association of
Psychoanalysis, 23, 93, 123
Yawm ad-Din, 44
Yves Duroux, 44
Zakir,18,21

Ingram Content Group UK Ltd.
Milton Keynes UK
UKHW020717260623
424053UK00014B/760